I0212038

A Tender Time

Quaker Voices on the End of Life

Patti Nesbitt, RN
Kristin Camitta Zimet

Baltimore Yearly Meeting

Copyright © 2024 Baltimore Yearly Meeting
All rights reserved.

ISBN: 979-8-218-42880-8

Copy Editor: Janaki Spickard Keeler
Book Design: Sarah Katreen Hoggatt, Book Layout Biz

Baltimore Yearly Meeting of the Religious Society of Friends
17100 Quaker Lane
Sandy Spring, MD 20860–1267
(301) 774-7663
https://www.bym-rsf.org

CONTENTS

To Our Readers

Dear Friends,

We all eventually face that tender time when we come to grips with mortality. Why do we call it tender? The end of life is a time when you are exposed and newly vulnerable, as a green shoot is tender; but given forthright, gentle handling, you can open to growth. This is a time when you can feel wounded and sensitive to touch, as a surgical site is tender; but given enough Light, your spirit heals. And this is a time that tests and confirms personal and corporate resolve to love one another tenderly, to become tenders of one another.

Tender comes from a root that means "to stretch," and this final stretch of life will surely stretch you. Whether mortality creeps up in slow aging or rips the rug out from under you, this time calls for steady faith and loving accompaniment.

In the language of early Friends, to be tender meant to be open and receptive to spiritual reality. Brian Drayton and William Taber tell us in *A Language for the Inward Landscape* that "tender" was one of George Fox's characteristic words, and he looked for tender people, especially during his seeking years, whenever he came into a new place.

Let us walk with you in this time. Death is not the enemy of life, nor the end of love; it can be a culmination and fulfillment of both. We want you to have the practical tools and spiritual supports you need to walk your path with confidence and grace. You can approach every step—emotional, practical, and legal—as an expression of Spirit.

There is nothing in this book to fear. Decline and death are natural occurrences that you can demystify and befriend. We offer a perspective of hope, wisdom, and assurance: a paradigm drawn from our Quaker heritage. Ours is a Spirit-led conviction that accepting death allows us to embrace life fully. We call on Friends to let our lives speak by loving one another all the way through. Let us follow our testimonies where they lead, so that we die as well as we live.

THE GENESIS OF THIS BOOK

This project came to life under the care of the End of Life Working Group of Baltimore Yearly Meeting. Our yearly meeting is a community of unprogrammed Friends across the mid-Atlantic region of the United States, including the District of Columbia and parts of Virginia, West Virginia, Pennsylvania, and Maryland. Although legalities vary across our jurisdictions, the Spirit does not. We trust that this book will speak to you wherever you are and whatever your faith.

The End of Life Working Group formed in 2019 to support Friends in late life and to gather resources addressing end of life issues. Group members are seasoned professionals in many fields, united in ministry to the aging. A growing chorus of voices around us tells us that this need is increasing in urgency.

Our working group is a subgroup of the Ministry and Pastoral Care Committee of Baltimore Yearly Meeting. Volunteers from ten monthly meetings across the yearly meeting joined in this collaboration. They are Lisa Allen, Julie Courtwright, Patricia LaNoue, Dave Morrison, Patti Nesbitt (clerk), Bob Rhudy, Margie Riley, Frances Schutz, Eileen Stanzione, John Surr, and Kristin Zimet. We honor John Surr's leadership in bringing this project to our attention and steadfastly insisting that we do it right.

This book began as an update of a document created in 2014 by Langley Hill Meeting in Virginia. Following the leadings of Spirit, it soon became far more. First intended for meetings in Virginia, the project grew to encompass the Baltimore Yearly Meeting, then the whole United States, then beyond. The book grew by leaps and bounds as materials poured in from Quaker social workers, lawyers, nurses, physicians, hospice chaplains, historians, funeral directors, and countless caregivers. We gathered experiences from meetings in the United States, the United Kingdom, Australia, and Aotearoa (New Zealand).

Several professionals provided guidance and insight from the perspective of their particular disciplines. We especially thank Deborah Boggs, Lauren Brownlee, Ellen Cronin, Sarah Gillooly, Bette Hoover, Callie Janoff, Joan Liversidge, Rich Liversidge, Carl Magruder, Terence McCormally, Margaret Boyd Meyer, and Tedford Taylor for substantial feedback and spiritual support.

We are grateful to the Friends Foundation for Aging for its generous support, which allows this book to reach more readers near and far. Thank you also to Janaki Spickard Keeler for her fine copy editing and Sarah Katreen Hoggatt for her design work. Their Quaker voices added insight and guidance.

THE STRUCTURE OF THE BOOK

We designed this book to move outward in widening circles, from the individual experience to the corporate. Every circle is about Love and Spirit. Every circle includes both grieving and grace. You can read straight through or go directly to any chapter you need.

Chapter 1 and Chapter 2 are about you. Chapter 1 guides you through the likely steps of aging, and Chapter 2 continues the story with the likely steps of dying. We lay out the processes in spiritual, biological, and practical terms, exploring typical patterns and how to meet them with grace. Our purpose is to offer you a chance to guide your own end and to make it full of meaning.

Chapter 3 is about your legacy. Use it as you decide what to give to the future and how to make those gifts secure. This is not only a matter of law, but a matter of the spirit.

Chapter 4 is for you as you undertake the role of primary caregiver, with its challenges and rewards. There is perhaps no greater gift. You will discover that you can, and you must, call on a great deal of support.

Chapter 5 is for you when you befriend a caregiver or a person in care. This spiritual and physical challenge can be an enormous blessing to both of you.

Chapter 6 is about ways your meeting as a whole can walk faithfully with those who are aging and dying. This process of pastoral care, as your meeting embraces it, will enrich the life of the entire meeting community.

All along the way, this book is about family, in the widest sense. You are born to one family, but families are also what you make—extended family, circles of friends, neighbors, and community. When we answer one another's needs, we form a larger, more resilient family. This is the essence of pastoral care.

Opening each chapter and woven throughout are the voices of Friends and others who are Quakerly in spirit. Quaker wisdom is corporate, so it feels fitting that far more than your two authors speak through our pages. We gathered words of wisdom both from long ago and just yesterday, from extensive reading and firsthand conversations. Anytime we mentioned that we were writing a book about the end of life, there came a perfect torrent of stories. If you are moved to find the context in which the voices spoke, go to "Finding the Voices" at the end of each chapter.

The shadow leaves that grace the book are reminders that each life is beautiful—in its individual form, in its partnership with light and with the tree of life, and in its time and manner of release.

The last part of the book is a Treasury of Resources. First, you will find three sets of questions to explore on your own or with your meeting. Next come checklists which many people begged us to include, covering actions to take after a death. The first checklist can guide survivors. Three more checklists help a meeting fulfill its overall role, coordinate a memorial meeting for worship, and create a memorial minute. "Readings and Support" follows—an annotated compilation of books, videos, websites, and more to widen your understanding and your base of support. Finally, there is a section to help you choose among ways to lay your body down and a model form on which Friends can record wishes for burial and commemoration.

No book can cover all possible wisdom about this universal experience. We have not dealt specifically with sudden death, suicide, violent death, drug overdose, or the death of young people. Nevertheless, you will find wisdom that applies to handling such situations tenderly. These important topics might be matters for a future edition.

Who We Are

This book is about you, and it is also about us. We have both been personally immersed in the issues it explores.

Patti is a retired palliative care nurse, caregiver, cancer survivor, mother, grandmother, author, clerk, traveling minister, and graduate of the School of the Spirit. Kristin is a poet, editor, caregiver, two-time cancer survivor, former EMT, patient care volunteer in hospice and in hospitals, Reiki master healer, mother, and grandmother. Patti is a member of Sandy Spring Friends Meeting in Maryland and Kristin is a member of Hopewell Centre Meeting in Virginia. We have both served on support committees for people who were aging and dying. We have shared a deep friendship for thirty years.

This book was slowly developed and seasoned. We waited on Guidance for next steps. We walked through illness and grief and gained perspective. We grappled with our own diminishments and embraced our own mortality. We grew in love and appreciation for one another, crying, laughing, and celebrating as we worked. Over and over we said to each other, "We are living this book!"

Our spouses, families, mentors, and spiritual friends are also alive in these pages. They have anchored us in the Light. Dear ones now deceased—John Zimet, Kristin's husband; Brian Hunt, Patti's boss at MedStar Montgomery Medical Center; and Betty Nesbitt, Patti's mother—guided us. We feel you, our readers, walking with us too, bringing our heartfelt work to fruition in your lives.

OUR PROCESS

How have we been able to spend so much time on these themes without succumbing to sadness? Yes, the work was often hard. It made us relive both losses and blessings. Sometimes we worked through tears, and we still cry for dear ones. But we have seen in our own lives the enduring and positive power of love. Our spiritual practices and love for each other also sustained us.

Together we read and reread every word out loud, testing it over and over. We returned and returned to maturing drafts, both over the phone and in person. We could agree to disagree, and did, but not as often as you might think. We wrestled lovingly, uncovering our own limitations and strengths, doubts and sureties. We toned each other down. We laughed a lot.

Our collaboration has been truly symbiotic. Patti's long involvement with Quaker process and her clinical experience combined well with Kristin's expertise in language and caregiving. Patti's research skill merged with Kristin's editorial savvy. Patti's prophetic zeal matched Kristin's readiness to play devil's advocate. Patti's Catholic upbringing and Kristin's Jewish heritage let us challenge each other's cultural assumptions—provoking, honoring, marveling, and surrendering in awe as we perceived another way.

Listening, questioning, and resting in uncertainty until way opened, we moved toward unity and service in the best Quaker sense. In short, this book is a work of love.

THE SPIRIT OF THIS BOOK

We are realists and optimists. We perceive that living well prepares us to die well, that everything we do is an expression of our spirit, and that the same is true for you. We trust that you have the potential to become an elder, one whose lived experience and ministry enriches the world.

The end of life is a time of tensions: you are pulled between physical and spiritual, losing and finding, diminishing and growing. We encourage you to live beautifully amid the tensions and the mysteries.

No one has the last word on how to live these years. We cannot be the last word on any topic, but we will rejoice if at times we open a way for you.

Let the voices gathered here help you consider tender possibilities. You will find your own voice and that of Spirit as you and your dear ones age. We hope to hear about your experiences and your responses to this book.

Take heart and walk with us now through your tender time.

In the Light,

Patti Nesbitt and *Kristin Camitta Zimet*
with the End of Life Working Group, Baltimore Yearly Meeting
January 2024

Finding the Voices

Brian Drayton and William P. Taber, Jr., *A Language for the Inward Landscape: Spiritual Wisdom from the Quaker Movement* (Philadelphia: Tract Association of Friends, 2016).

Completing Your Life: Spirit-Led Aging

What is it you plan to do
With your one wild and precious life?
—Mary Oliver, 1992

Accept with serenity the approach of each new stage of life. Welcome the approach of old age, both for oneself and for others, as an opportunity for wisdom, for detachment from turmoil, and for greater attachment to the Light.
—Philadelphia Yearly Meeting *Faith and Practice*, 2017

Dying well is a lifelong work, and its skills must be learned while one is still healthy and vigorous.
—William Z. Shetter, 2012

Although growing older may bring increasing disability and loneliness, it can also bring serenity, detachment, and wisdom. Pray that in your final years you may be enabled to find new ways of receiving and reflecting God's love.
—Baltimore Yearly Meeting *Resource for Faith and Practice*, 2013

If we are not trained in a trust of mystery and some degree of
tolerance for ambiguity and suffering, we will not proceed very far
on the spiritual journey.

—Richard Rohr, 2024

I am learning to offer to God my days and my nights, my joy, my
work, my pain and my grief.... I am learning to use the time I have
more wisely.... And I am learning to forget at times my puritan
conscience which prods me to work without ceasing, and instead,
to take time for joy.

—Elizabeth Watson, 1979

I believe eternal life is in each moment of life, here and now; the
real tragedy is not how or when we die but if we do not live the life
we are given to our full potential.

—Jenifer Faulkner, 1982

Each morning is new now. I wake to the inner music of thanks for
the dear gift of life....

—Bradford Smith, 1965

LATE LIGHT, PHOTOGRAPHERS TELL US, IS the richest light of
all. In the hour before the sun sets, it imbues the landscape
with depth and warmth. This is a dynamic and fleeting time. So
too, in the last years of your life, your inner light begins to shift.
New wavelengths prevail, slower and more beautiful. You can approach your life with greater clarity and tenderness.

If you let divine Light in, your later years can open you to love's
mature fullness. You can make your peace with old issues and draw
people close. This can be a time for accelerated growth of spirit, and
your experience can light the way for others. Regardless of your financial security or physical vitality, you can come into your own as an elder.

In many cultures, the older you get, the more valuable you are. Elders carry wisdom, heritage, and vision. It is good to think of yourself in this way. Even if your physical world shrinks, you can expand spiritually, socially, and creatively. Your life is part of a much bigger story, some of which you can shape to the end. You always have choices in how you respond to change. You make your own meaning.

More strongly than ever, these years ask you to live the Quaker testimonies. Some identities and possessions and attachments fall away. These years invite simplicity—perhaps in the form of downsizing, retiring, or slowing. They urge stewardship, in how you choose to spend the time and resources that remain. They heighten your need to dwell in community and to make peace while there is time. They reveal your equality with all other beings who are mortal. Above all, these years summon you to the testimony of integrity, standing in the truth of a changing body and soul.

LIVING NEW PATTERNS

Each person, if granted enough time, ages in a unique way. But there are typical patterns of change—mental, physical, practical, and spiritual. If you are aware of such patterns, you can take stock of where you are. You can anticipate change and adapt with grace. In *The Art of Dying Well*, Katy Butler puts it this way: "People who are willing to contemplate their aging, vulnerability, and mortality often live better lives in old age and illness, and experience better deaths, than those who don't."

Changing Mind
You might stay keen-minded to the end. Physical exercise, nutritious food, good sleep, and mental activity can help keep up your edge. But usually with age, people undergo a slow pattern of cognitive shift.

You begin to misplace things, though they do turn up in logical places. You enter a room and pause a moment to remember why.

Your reflexes are not quite what they used to be. More and more, names and words you know perfectly well take time to surface. Your mind, like your body, needs more rest.

Acknowledge these changes. They are not necessarily something to worry about. They might be part of a softening in how you perceive things. You are turning from preoccupation with details to a vision of your life as a whole. If so, this change could be a component of developing wisdom.

Your mental changes might be part of the larger work of letting go. Could it be that your brain wants you to relax into a gentler rhythm? That your spirit is asking you to devote yourself to less worldly things?

Everybody feels at least a twinge of fear about forgetfulness. Is it dementia? The testimonies of stewardship and integrity call you to face this question head-on. Ask trusted friends your age whether they are experiencing the same things. Tell your doctors about any unusual changes. Maybe they will rule out the possibility of disease and set your mind at ease. If not, you will give yourself the most time possible to gather resources and come to terms with what is happening.

No matter whether changes are benign or serious, you can make legal and financial provision now for the future that you want, while you are clear-minded and articulate.

Changing Body

If you have been living with a physical challenge for a long time, even from birth, the level and type of challenge are likely to increase with age. In that case, you do have a head start in learning to cope with grace. You might find this lets you show the way to others.

If you live with a degenerative disease, you are accustomed to physical change. Heart failure, dementia, Parkinson's, and many other conditions take years to unfold. You become skillful at adapting to diminishments.

But even if you are in fine condition, you can expect your physical ability to decline at some point. As William Shetter describes, new impairments "require more and more resolution to contend with."

One way to perceive physical decline with age is as a sequence. The following four steps are based on the work of Katy Butler. Nobody experiences every single detail, but see whether you can find your place here:

1. In *early aging*, queries about aging begin to arise in you. Perhaps that is why you picked up this book. Minor health issues increase, and it takes longer to recover. Your hearing and sight change; it's harder to hear high notes and to see at night. The side effects of poor habits and medical treatments in the past catch up with you and leave you with a bad back, gut issues, or cardiovascular challenges.

   A restful, quiet time during the day is welcome. Upkeep of things begins to be more tiring. It takes more diligent effort to maintain health.

2. *A little later*, you want more time for inner stillness. You feel a pull to downsize or move. You have more medical specialists—a cardiologist, physical therapist, and so on. You take more medications. You are less physically resilient, and you exercise at a slower pace. Maybe you start to need a cane or a walker.

3. *Greater changes* follow. You are called to "hallow your diminishments," in the words of John Yungblut. You are advised to stop driving. You can't keep up with ordinary activities and routines. You need increasing help to stand, and you rely on handrails, grab bars, or other equipment. You consider a home health aide or assisted living. Your doctor uses terms like "progressive," "serious," "advanced," "end stage," and "goals of care."

4. With *advancing difficulties*, your physical needs multiply, and you want more support for body and spirit. You have lost significant weight. You walk limited distances, and you sleep a lot. You turn fully from "doing" to "being."

A second, quite different way to perceive physical decline is in terms of timing. Here are three separate scenarios:

1. The first scenario is *sudden*. Your physical decline remains mild, your symptoms manageable. You continue to work and play, perhaps for years. Then comes a catastrophic event—for example, a major heart attack. You have to make an abrupt, enormous adjustment.
2. A second scenario is *episodic*. A series of emergencies lands you in the hospital. Each crisis leaves you less able; it adds frailty and taxes the will to live. One example of this pattern is a series of small strokes.
3. A third scenario is a *slow fade*. This can be a hard ride or a gentle one. There might be an underlying condition such as congestive heart failure or dementia, or just a long period of increasing frailty.

We cannot know how much time we have. Most of us say we want a quick, sudden death, in our sleep, without pain. Only 8 percent of us get this wish granted, but there are gifts in slower timing. There is time to adjust to the news, time to put your affairs in order, and time to do the inner work your soul yearns to complete.

There is a positive way to regard your physical condition. At ninety-two, Mary Morrison urged, "Don't waste a moment feeling sorry for what you can no longer do. Just be thankful for what your body will still do for you."

Changing Work

Changing mind and body often call for a transition in your work. Maybe you approach work with a new perspective. Things that were once compelling lose their fascination, and you long to lavish time on a different set of things.

Your energy shifts. You don't have the drive or stamina to work day and night. Maybe your body is less and less up to the demands of your job. Maybe you dream of retiring. If you cannot retire, you find yourself longing to work at a more comfortable pace and you envision a fallback plan. If you scramble to make ends meet, you call increasingly upon determination to keep going.

If your income allows, perhaps you choose to continue working in an altered form, to bring your work to a satisfying close, or to pass your accomplishments to the next generation. Perhaps in the time that remains, you are excited to reach for new work of which you have always dreamed—or never dreamed. For example, Anne Felton writes that just after she retired, her husband was diagnosed with Alzheimer's. She received a "prompting" to study spiritual direction, something she had never heard of before.

Maybe, because of your age, you are let go from your job unwillingly. Maybe new technology displaces you or daunts you, and age makes it hard to find comparable work. Willing or not, part of your identity was wrapped up in the work you did, and it is stripped away. This is a profound shakeup. Out of the emptiness, you are challenged to create new fullness and meaning.

Changing Soul

Typically, when physical and mental changes take us to the edge of our comfort zones, the soul is challenged too. We are forced to confront limitations and to question ingrained responses. This is where God seems to work with us most, and where we have the greatest potential to grow.

Patterns of physical change have spurred spiritual transitions your whole life long. When someone cut your umbilical cord, you discovered that it was possible to breathe on your own. An implicit quest began, to know yourself as separate yet still part of a larger whole. Such soul work arises at every age—infant, toddler, teenager, young adult, and so on. But often it becomes most palpable and active when time and energy are running out. Whatever lifelong issue has beset you, whatever has been a recurrent theme in your life, is laid bare.

For example, one Friend realized she had always struggled to believe she was worthy of love. "Can I trust that Love will catch me as I fall into old age? Will Love be there to receive me when I die? Can I learn to say, with the psalmist, 'I shall not want'?" She began to wrestle actively with this spiritual challenge.

Another Friend saw he had always needed to be the one in charge. "Can I let someone else take care of me?" he wondered. "How much power do I have left? Can I say, 'Thy will be done'?"

Your sense of your own uniqueness increases with age. As the poet May Sarton wrote in her later years, "Now I become myself." And at the same time, if you allow it, your spiritual perspective is widening. Beyond the confines of your own life, you see yourself enmeshed in the whole web of life. Moving beyond, you glimpse yourself united with the cosmos.

For some people, as the body grows frail, the spirit grows stronger. "I have become very much aware of the supremacy of the spirit over the body, in principle," wrote Walter Martin in the year before his death. "Although I have failed to achieve this idea in practice, my real self, namely the spiritual, has been considerably enhanced.... God has strengthened my faith, for I feel that it is simply the start of a new life."

As time runs out, soul work grows strenuous and urgent. You foresee surrendering the whole of yourself—to what? Will you surrender to the All, or to nothingness?

Responding to Losses

Amid these patterns of change, there is difficult news and encouraging news. If the glass empties with age, it also fills.

Here is the hard part, the difficult news right up front: in elder years, grieving is fairly inescapable. Even if you yourself remain robust, you grieve for friends and family who are aging and dying around you. Your original circle of companions is probably growing smaller. Fewer people share a past with you, a past that is now rich and substantial but increasingly invisible. If you leave work, you lose colleagues who made up part of your social world. Fewer people know every part of you, from way back when to now. It often takes more effort than it used to take to make yourself known and form new friendships. You have to deal with loneliness.

If you are older than your siblings or partner, you might find yourself slowing down by comparison; if you are younger, you might see others slowing down. Either way, you mourn the old equality of energy, the old contexts of shared adventure. It is common to grieve for your own health, strength, and stamina, as well as for theirs.

Maybe you are still vigorous, but people start to assume you shouldn't be invited on that hike or that you will sit out the soccer game. Or maybe they do include you as always, and halfway up the mountain you have to sit down. You begin to budget your energy, devoting yourself to a narrowed number of activities. This in itself grievously shrinks your circle and your sense of participation in life.

You might mourn the lessening of independence. Someone else balances your checkbook or runs your errand or drives you to the doctor—or you can see that day approaching. Maybe you wonder whether anyone will step in as those needs increase. You might have to learn to ask.

You were the giver, the one who offered an arm, baked for the sale, or fixed the sink for a homebound neighbor. Now you are more often the receiver; you cast about for possible ways to give. You know yourself as the doer; now you must try to describe yourself by other measures. Who is this person you are becoming?

You grieve too for the things that you foresee you are going to miss. Maybe you really wanted to be part of your great-grandson's life. Maybe you finally admit you will never see the Grand Canyon, something you always promised yourself to see. Or you simply know this could be the last time you will dance till dawn or stack a winter's firewood single-handedly.

You might grieve the vanishing cultural context of your generation. You push yourself to stay "with it," or you feel increasingly out of sync, defending "the old ways." You might feel less visible than when you were young, less valued or beautiful or sexy.

You might miss the pull of activities that once had meaning for you and filled your life to overflowing. You might mourn the old collections you don't have energy or will to maintain, or the person who thought they were so important.

You grieve the lost sense of having limitless time. Looking back, you grieve the mistakes that made less-than-perfect use of the time behind you.

All these griefs might show up as depression. If you look closely, you might find anger, too. As the poet Dylan Thomas put it, many of us "do not go gentle into that good night," but "rage, rage against the dying of the light." Perhaps you are angry at your body for starting to fail you; at illness, and at doctors who can only help so much; and at God, who seems to be letting you down. It is common to be angry at your family for managing you or marginalizing you or living on without you. Deep down, you could even be angry at the kind person who effortlessly shovels your snow, a task that leaves you sore and breathless.

Perhaps underneath it all is fear. You might fear frailty, pain, dementia, or the unknown. Your childhood prayers take on a different meaning. One Friend notes, "'Now I lay me down to sleep, I pray the Lord my soul to keep' suddenly sounds a little ominous. 'Holy Mary, Mother of God, pray for us sinners now and at the hour of our death' is starting to seem all too explicit."

Remember being a teenager, wracked by growing pains, wondering who you are becoming? Getting old takes getting used to. The longer you live, the more the challenge. Be kind and affectionate toward yourself as you grow up, and seek out others who treat you that way.

Grief, anger, and fear are normal, real responses to letting go. They deserve recognition. It helps to unpack them and talk about them; you will find plenty of company.

Recall that the glass is also half full. You do not have to dwell upon negatives. There is a whole other way to respond.

Let go of people who see age as a liability, or simply stop believing them. You don't need to change their minds. Occasionally, shake your head and laugh at yourself. Cultivate joy, and surround yourself with people who can support it. Live in a climate that includes hope.

Hannah Whitall Smith writes of that hope: "I am convinced it is a great art to know how to grow old gracefully, and I am determined to practise it.... It is so delicious to be *done* with things.... I am tremendously content to let one activity after another go, and to wait quietly and happily the opening of the door at the end of the passage-way that will let me in to my real abiding place."

Your responses to loss are not fixed. "As long as I've lived," says one eighty-year-old Friend, "I am still a work in progress. I just keep growing up." Your feelings will certainly change as you go on aging. Meanwhile, naming them will let you move forward with the practical decisions of aging well.

Deciding Where to Live

One of the biggest questions as you age is where to live. Begin now by taking a fearless inventory.

Think two years ahead. It can take two years to find a place and move. Is it reasonable to imagine you will be up to living here two years from now?

Taking Stock

Start with a physical inventory. Consider your own body and that of anyone who lives with you. What changes are clearly coming? Is it still comfortable to live here? How have you begun to feel about the tall flight of stairs, the big garden to weed, the long walk to the mailbox? Can you get easily into the attic or basement, the high cupboard or the stuffed closet? Are you using the whole of your home, or are you keeping more and more to certain rooms? Are you using all your things, or does it feel like you live, as one Friend puts it, "in a museum of your life"?

What about your social needs? Is your location close enough to family and friends, should your energy lessen? Is this a beloved neighborhood, or have your friends moved away? Do you interact with your neighbors? Do you still need that space for parties and for grown children? Can you get easily to activities, stores, and health providers? Could you reach them if you stopped driving?

Now come emotional questions: Do you feel safe here? Does your home express the person you are today, or the person you used to be? Does it fit the person you expect to become in the next few years? How attached are you to the history embedded here? Are you lonely or fulfilled here? Are you near the people who are dearest to you? Would you give a lot just to stay here—or would you give a lot just to get away? If you wait five years and then move, will you have the energy to make new friends and a new life? Do you catch yourself daydreaming of a different place or way of life?

There are financial questions, too: Does your home give you as much in pleasure as it takes from you in cost and upkeep? Will your income remain high enough to support you here? How would you have to budget in order to stay? If you share your home now, and the other person died, could you manage the cost alone? Where else could you afford to live?

Aging in Place

If enough of your answers are positive, it makes sense to keep aging in place. Using your answers, modify your home to match your current abilities and enthusiasms. Then, remembering that you could experience a sudden drop in ability, go further. Make provision well ahead of time, and you won't have to do it under pressure or in crisis. Such actions don't mean giving up and giving in. They are gifts to your present and future self.

Aging well in place requires you to make decisions. It means you gradually clear away possessions that just sit on the shelf or drain your energy instead of giving joy. "Cleaning out my closet was like watching my life flash before my eyes," one Friend recalls. "All that teen angst, all the old passions. I got to replay and enjoy it, and then I found I didn't need to keep most of the props, the paraphernalia of memory. The parts of the past that matter are inside me, deeply ingrained in the person I am now."

Once you have made room, physically and psychologically, you can prepare for one-floor living. A first priority is to create a bedroom and full bath at the level where you enter the house, to use now or eventually. You might prefer self-regulating lighting and ventilation, so you need not keep opening and shutting windows and doors. In the bathroom, you might install high toilet seats and a walk-in shower with grab bars and room for a shower chair. You might put levers on doors and faucets instead of knobs.

An open floor plan with wide paths and doorways is desirable to get around with a walker or wheelchair. Cabinets with drawers replacing the lower shelves make bending over less challenging.

Surfaces easy to reach and clean make maintenance easier. Outdoors, you might install a ramp suitable for crutches, a walker, or a wheelchair.

It is wise to stock your medicine cabinet and your pantry well in case accident or illness grounds you. To help with memory problems, you can label contents of refrigerators, drawers, and cabinets.

A vital element of aging in place is fall prevention. Falling is a fact of life as we grow older—not if, but when and how often. It is a good idea to create non-slip surfaces for entryways and stairs. Tack down loose carpet and eliminate trip hazards like throw rugs and wires. Go for bright lighting, mark steps with high contrast, consider handrails in the hallway, and update your prescriptions for eyeglasses.

Then exercise! Balance exercises will keep you upright and increase the flexibility and strength of feet and ankles. Building upper-body strength will help you pull yourself up from a fall or break your fall without breaking bones. Weight-bearing exercises will build bones, strengthen muscles, and improve endurance. All of these reduce frailty and ensure safety for living at home.

Aging in place also means letting go of the idea that you can and must do it all for yourself. What is the most taxing task you do? Can you afford to pay someone to take trash to the dump or clean your house? What services does your community offer? What capable friends can you count on? Who can stand on a ladder or run an errand? Extend yourself to know your neighbors and build a community of mutual aid. Start developing a written list of where to find support. Start accustoming yourself to using that list.

Play "what if" to plan your way out of difficulties before they arise. The purpose is to prepare for the worst while you hope for the best. The idea is not to scare yourself, but to advance with confidence. What if you fall—is it time to wear an emergency call button? What if an ambulance comes—have you posted your medications? What if you are lying unconscious—does somebody routinely check on you?

A different approach to aging in place is to open your home to someone who helps with meals, errands, chores, and companionship. Some Friends convert a basement or an unused bedroom to affordable housing. For one couple that had lived in cohousing, this was an easy transition. They had a capable younger friend who was nearly homeless. They offered him an outbuilding in trade for renovations, yard work, and repairs. They enjoy his skills and his company.

Not least, recognize any bargain you are making with yourself, spoken or secret. "I will stay here as long as I can stand on my own two feet." "I will live in this house as long as my grandson needs refuge." One Friend found himself "too old to do yard work" after a knee replacement. He could have hired help, but this was the deal-breaker which "forced him" to move. Another Friend decided to age at home, assured that his family could help him shower, eat, and dress. He drew the line at letting his family clean him if he suffered fecal incontinence.

It can be difficult to imagine "what might be" when you are still embedded in "what is." Still, what change would release you from living in your present home? Figure out your next move well ahead of that potential time.

Relocating

Is it time to move? Suppose your inventory shows that all these preparations are not enough. You find that your house already takes too much energy or money, or you suspect that in a year or two, it will. You doubt it will still feel comfortable or safe. Maybe you foresee growing isolated or uneasy or depressed there. You want to devote yourself next to something this living space does not support. You want everything you love to do within closer reach. This nest is too big. It is time to relocate.

Any move—whether to a larger or a smaller space—is a goodbye; it entails some disconnection and sadness. It is also a hello—an opportunity to affirm and reinvent who you are. You are not your address and you are not your lifestyle. You are not the things you own; your memories are embedded not in objects, but in your spirit. You can't help taking with you your whole history, what shaped you and what matters most. And if you allow it, even in a smaller space, you can't help growing.

A move costs a lot. It entails hard work, both physical and emotional. But it is also a chance to review and reshape your life. Relocating is best done while there is plenty of time and energy to do it right and to form new bonds in a new setting.

Your options might be wide open or narrow, depending on income, health, and geography.

The most expensive option is a Continuing Care Retirement Community (CCRC). A CCRC gives residents care from independent living to assisted living to nursing care to the end. This is your "last move." You might move to different units within the community, but your care and context are assured. You live in a separate "place of your own," yet you are enmeshed with other people and watched over. If you look at a CCRC, ask about amenities like meals, entertainment, activities, shared gardens, a pool, an art studio, trails, and transportation to shopping and medical centers. Ask whether it requires a major investment up front and whether they offer a refund if you leave or die.

It can take years to get situated in a CCRC, so it is vital to get on the list early. You can accept or refuse offers until you are ready and the available space is right. Expect a financial and medical assessment when you apply and when you accept.

The least expensive option is moving in with family. One way to do this is to create an apartment in the basement, so you live both with the family and apart. The emotional costs and benefits of living with family are hard to quantify. At its best, this solution means being among people both familiar and dear, building intergenerational bonds. The challenges are to fit into the family's routine and lifestyle, and to maintain harmony. The dynamics of a visit are different from those of living together.

Even if you have a close-knit family, you won't see yourself exactly the way your family sees you. It is important to air expectations on both sides with radical honesty. As your needs grow, family might find themselves untrained in giving care. It is likely that at some point, issues of dependency and role reversal will call for kindness and forbearance on everyone's part.

Boundaries are important in this setting. Even when you love someone dearly, close quarters create friction. Be sensitive to the space and dignity of one another. Boundaries might have to change as your needs change.

Another issue is mutuality. One Friend living with her son has gladly taken over after-school care for her grandsons. Another helps out with the mortgage; she pays a fraction of what it costs to live alone, but it is a welcome contribution. Yet another instituted progressive dinners that begin with the main course upstairs in her daughter's dining room and end with dessert downstairs in her own living room. With ingenuity, you can make sure giving flows in both directions.

Other solutions fall between living in a CCRC and living with family. There are many Quaker retirement communities, four of them within Baltimore Yearly Meeting's region alone. You might join a cohousing community or intentional community such as ElderSpirit in Abingdon, Virginia. You might choose a small group home, share a home with friends in the same situation, or invite a person to live with you in return for care. Each of these solutions has challenges, and each keeps you independent and has the potential reward of new connections.

Remember that all your life you have practiced adapting. The challenges of your elder years are no greater than the ones you solved at any turning point—as a newborn, a teenager, or an adult in midlife.

Wherever you go—whether to a venue full of enrichment or to reduced circumstances—you are still going to be you. One Friend who loved parties found himself a lonely widower in assisted living. He started a monthly poetry reading, which he emceed; it drew a hundred residents. Another Friend with a forceful personality wound up in a wheelchair in an overcrowded nursing home. There she "adopted" her timid roommate, and she advocates loudly and effectively for her friend's care. Wherever you move, your spirit can shine.

BECOMING MORE

Aging does mean letting go, but not becoming less. It hides the possibility of great gifts—if you seek them out. If you are fortunate, you get the gift of time: time at last to listen, heal, and pray, and foremost, to love.

More Affection

Age offers the gift of self-knowledge. The weight of accumulated experience presses you to take stock. You have time to face your fears, your avoidances, your inner limitations—and break through to understanding.

If you take that gift, age offers the second gift of self-acceptance. You can open to love, beginning with loving yourself. You are done striving for the achievements your society and family and social set prescribe. You shrug aside the stereotypes of what it means to age. You can accept what you are and even laugh about it. John Yungblut even suggests that your foibles, failures, and diminishments can become companions and teachers, owned with a certain detached lightness of heart.

Once you love yourself, you need not project your unlove onto others. And now that you have "seen it all," very little alarms or disgusts you anymore. From inside and outside, you know about frailty, woundedness, and healing. You discover it is easy to let others into the garden that is big enough for everyone.

Yes, your old circle of people is shrinking. For that reason, it is time to let tenderness for those who remain come to the fore. You still have time to recognize and dwell in the full light of connections. If you do, the elder years can be the sweetest of all.

Chances are you have deepened over the years, so you have perspective. You give up shallow acquaintances; you know who really cares for you and whom you really care for. It is time finally to release old grudges, give up old jealousies, and resolve old wrongs. Then you breathe easier. You find fresh ways to relate.

Who is right there in plain sight, with love to give and receive? Who are you not yet seeing—a shy grandchild, a struggling neighbor, the grocery store cashier? You might find your losses prompt you to new friendships in unexpected places. Where can you make "an opening meet for heaven," as the poet Charles Williams called it, right here and now?

Mainstream culture claims that your value is based on what you earn and produce. This prejudice is hard on seniors, and it is contrary to what every faith tells you. You not only have that of God within you, but it can shine brighter the older you get. Never presume that others don't need you, that you are becoming useless.

A surprising number of people around you are pining for real connection. You have a great deal of common ground with others your own age, who are also experiencing changes and losing friends. Communities of older people capitalize on this fact. But why limit your friendships to the same age? Look also to younger people.

You bring perspective and time to listen, two enormous gifts. Young people need you, first, as a mentor; even if they have a solid family, it takes more than one mother and more than one father to bring up a whole person. Second, they need you as a friend. Friendships arise between people of any age.

After all, you hold the memories of every age you have been. Somewhere in you persists a two-year-old, a thirteen-year-old, a fifty-year-old, and more, open to mutual delight. Having friends of every age keeps all of them alive.

If you are unpartnered now, open also to the possibility of new love. There are countless examples. One Friend fell in love at eighty-six with another Friend of ninety-four. They held a ceremony of commitment in the manner of Friends, which allowed them to affirm permanent partnership while keeping their legal and financial status separate. Another pair in a Quaker retirement house got permission to take down the wall between their two apartments.

Connection will give you more than emotional and spiritual satisfaction. The more widely you connect, and the more tenderly you interact, the more likely it is that you will stay physically healthy.

More Purpose

At every age you need purpose. Sometimes life throws a new purpose at you. You become the caregiver for your grandchildren or for your parents. You lose your job or your savings or your house and must start over from scratch. Even should none of these sudden changes arise, aging brings abundant possibilities of new purpose.

If you are older than others around you, you are automatically a way-finder. Whether you realize it or not, others are constantly learning from you. They are absorbing your version of what it means to age. Years from now, your image will come back to them. Will your example limit them, or will it light their way?

You too have witnessed many models of how to age, and you carry those possibilities. One of your purposes now is to look at them. Are you in awe of how your grandfather spent his later years, or distressed about it? Either way, the experience has gifts of insight for you. Will you follow your family's usual path? Will you walk a new and better path?

Being a positive way-finder can be a conscious choice. It doesn't mean hiding worry or pain behind a facade. It does mean staying vital in spirit. Show those around you how to live as fully and as well as you can until you die.

You can seek fresh purpose in service. Can you reinvent yourself, so you are not just pulling back (the literal meaning of "retire") but moving forward? If you enjoyed your work, what was the most rewarding element—solving problems, building something solid, uplifting people? Your joy can lead you to new purpose. A former waitress organizes a soup kitchen. A truck driver takes rescue dogs from Texas to Pennsylvania. A construction worker builds a Habitat for Humanity house. A retired doctor runs a vaccination clinic.

Senior volunteers seem to be the heart and soul of most communities; they power a gift economy, based not on money but on generous time and attention. Organizations are waiting to connect you with others in heartfelt and valuable ways: reading to children in after-school settings, answering a crisis hotline, sponsoring a refugee family. Indeed, why limit yourself to human beings? One Friend takes care of a feral cat colony; another facilitates a native plant exchange. You can open your heart in volunteer activities for any interest and for any level of mobility.

Maybe there is an opportunity now for work you never got to do. One Friend who regretted not having worked in health care began to volunteer at a hospital. Another Friend wished his career had been in social work. He got a real estate license and began helping people with low income buy a first home.

New gifts can even arise out of diminishments. One sculptor who worked in heavy marble lost her strength; she began to pour gold into tiny forms, casting lost wax jewelry. One Olympic athlete lost the use of his legs. From a wheelchair; he began to teach seated yoga. This kind of transformation can be subtle. A man who had held audiences spell-bound nearly lost his voice to cancer; he whispered wonderful jokes.

Reflect upon all the things you are doing for free. Which are essential or genuine pleasures? Which are obligations you fulfill just out of habit or courtesy, and which are true ministry? Listen deeply, and you will know which activities to keep pursuing. Howard Thurman advises, "Ask yourself what makes you come alive, and go do that, because what the world needs is people who have come alive."

You are alive! New joys are possible. One woman decided to try a new skill every year on her birthday. At seventy-seven, she learned to tango. At seventy-eight, she tried wind surfing. She is keeping the family in suspense about what she will do at eighty. The choice certainly will depend on her health. She could venture to put on a virtual reality headset, or take up drumming, or learn to count in Chinese. Her spirit is bound to come up with something new, however wild or gentle. What would you do in her place?

When time and energy start to feel limited and you foresee an end to them, don't shut down. Some people contract into chronic anxiety, withdrawing from activity or doling out energy. But some people make the most of every moment, greeting it with surprise, pleasure, and gratitude. You can make this a purposeful practice.

Bradford Smith reflects in his journal, "Today's dawn, since it may be the last, comes with all the force and newness of the first, and so eternity is bent within the arc of personal experience. So time, though it threatens the great erasure, is itself erased."

As you age—letting go of some activities, no longer rushing from one engagement to another—whatever you do gains focus and significance. You are like a sculptor, cutting away a block of stone to find the beautiful form within.

You can invite light to shine on whatever you get to do. Approached with purpose, even basic acts—seeing a sunrise, putting on a new shirt, finding the first crocus—are not taken for granted. If you eat less, you remember how good it is to hunger and then to eat. If you talk less, deep conversation becomes a prize; you remember how good it is to touch minds. If walking becomes harder, and you go not quite so far, maybe each step is a purposeful touch down onto earth, an affirmation. If you tire readily, maybe you discover, for the first time in a hectic life, the beauty of rest.

If it is harder to move—taking care not to fall, carrying less, driving less—you might also find yourself more able to travel in another sense. You range across the arc of your life, with access to a whole atlas there. You gather and label the pictures of those wide vistas, literally or figuratively. You reach across time and space to the people who have meant a lot to you. With ease, you hold others—individuals, groups, the whole earth—in the Light.

London Yearly Meeting expressed this purpose beautifully in 1923:

> Those of you who are kept by age or sickness from more active work, who are living retired lives, may in your very separation have the opportunity of liberating power for others. Your prayers and thoughts go out further than you think, and as you wait in patience and in communion with God, you may be made ministers of peace and healing and be kept young in soul.

More Spirit

The elder years test your faith and give you time to remake it. Some people struggle with old habits of faith. They reach in accustomed ways for the Divine and come up empty. Others feel Love drawing them near; they begin to perceive that of God more readily than ever.

You might "know" things more instinctively, not at an intellectual remove. Guidance arrives with less effort. There is a surety, the way a baker's hands know when the bread is kneaded enough, or the way some people cook without recipes. You are open to mystery, familiar with the depths, and ready to risk. Answers are richer, no longer simple yes or no but multifaceted, mysterious, and open-ended. You have stability; you have been rounded out in life's tumblers, enriched by ambiguity, tempered by illness, strengthened by darkness, and grounded in God's love.

Your thinking tends to become more universal. One Friend says, "At the market, I am lost without my list. But I always glow with awareness of how many unknown people work so that I can eat." William Shetter says it this way: "There are fewer and fewer things that truly matter. The years have accumulated such a store of inner lasting value that I no longer feel the weight of the perishable.... My life is becoming intensely focused on presence and Presence."

There is finally enough soul time—time to rest, season, delve, and dream. There is time to try out spiritual practices and let them heal old hurts; there is time to turn regularly inward toward Spirit. Earlier Friends called this attention to Spirit "retirement." Margaret Guenther calls it "the monastery of old age."

Less distracted by social norms, obligations, and belongings, you might find it easier to "rest a while" in reflection and prayer. Though your body is slowing down, in reciprocal motion, your spirit moves more freely. You have more time and space to devote to your Inward Teacher. You might come to a point, according to Douglas Steere, where you "stop praying and begin to be prayed in."

Dorothy Steere writes:

As I grow older, I seem to need more time for inner still-ness.... This can happen in the midst of daily chores or when walking in a crowd or riding in a train. It means being still, open, reflective, holding within myself the crucible of joy and pain of all the world, and lifting it up to God. Praise comes into it, and thankfulness for all the love I have known and shared, the realization of how much of the time I am carried, supported, upheld by others and the love of God.

The quietude you discover was there underneath all along—but once it might have seemed boring or threatening or empty, so you covered it over with action. Now you reach for its rich gifts: relaxation, awareness, patience, insight, and peace. You could embody these qualities in a discipline such as meditation, tai chi, qigong, or yoga. Or you could simply live into them, until as Thích Nhất Hạnh suggested, "Peace is every step."

With quietude, you put yourself at the disposal of Spirit. In that yielding, your prophetic voice can rise. Becoming what Margery Post Abbott calls "an everyday prophet," you perceive and name the world as it is—from large events to microaggressions. You bear active witness when events unfold for the better or for the worse.

Looking at your own life, you can become convinced that beyond each loss a love has continued to hold. You reframe your life, discovering that something beyond human was always at work there.

As you come closer to death, your life story bends toward completion. One Friend moved through a long hard process of inner simplification, until only the deepest part of her mattered. She said, "In illness, I realized that Love is at the core of it all."

TELLING YOUR STORY

Early Friends seldom lived much past their forties or fifties. Today, if you have good access to medical care, you might live far longer. You have time to fulfill your possibilities and make meaning of your life. You have time to tell your story, make it right, and bring it to completion.

The later years give you perspective. Your story belongs both to a large context of world events mostly beyond your control and to intimate events your choices shaped. Your genes, your family history, and your social setting are givens, but it is your ultimate response to them that matters. You now tell your story as you never told it before. You do not make up what happened, but you do get to choose how you assign significance.

There are many ways to get your story flowing. It might help to meditate and journal every day. It might help to find a really good listener. You might start recording on your phone, or send a series of email sketches, or draft letters to a real or imaginary friend. You could make handwritten drawings and notes for somebody to digitize or transcribe.

You might try storyboarding, something professional storytellers do. Storyboarders write down pieces of the story on strips of paper and rearrange them till the meaning flows. You can even tack scraps to the wall or to a board. This process is a bit like designing a quilt.

Your story is not as fixed as you think. There are many ways to tell the "same" story. Don't settle for someone else's version; no one can get it right but you. When two sisters describe their childhood, one begins, "Mother never cared for children." The other says, "Mother adored us." These premises have quite unlike consequences. If an old version of your story was crippling, you don't have to give it power anymore. You do not deny it—you transform it.

One Friend, writing her story, put in big capital letters, "So I never went to Australia!" After each life event, she wrote it again, accusingly. This missed opportunity undercut all the things she actually had done. Staring at the loss hogging the page, at last she decided to pray. "When your angel comes to take me to heaven," she found herself praying, "could we please take a detour and stop in Australia? I've earned it!" With this happy ending, she transformed her entire story. Australia became not a failure, but a culmination.

Let the story change you in the telling; let it shift your future. You can make peace with the past—speak your truth, forgive others, ask for forgiveness, and forgive yourself. You can reach for reconciliation with people from whom you have been estranged. You can accept yourself and seek reconnection with others. You can fulfill promises you made to yourself and take up gifts you did not claim before. In all these ways you are freed to move forward.

Eventually, it is time to share that story with people you care about. Perhaps you craft a memoir, make a video interview, or write a long letter for your grandchildren. Now you will not disappear—you will become known. Your personal life will continue beyond your own lifetime, overflowing into the lives of others. It will guide the young. It will lengthen the line of your family's history, too, relaying legends to coming generations.

Age makes you a living time link, a memory keeper for family, friends, and community. You are the conscious bearer of a stretch of world history and the culmination of past generations. You hold direct source material nobody else knows, and you have hard-earned wisdom that is distinctly yours. Never doubt that sharing your insight is crucial to ongoing creation. Your voice is of great value.

Your story is still continuing to develop. In youth it was important to take hold, assemble resources, and gain control. In age it became important to let go—of possessions, activities, friends, health, even life itself. Now your story shows you arriving at a quite different fullness. You are entering a new, less physical dimension, one a younger person might never imagine.

Listening to the story ever more attentively, you hear what attachment to your past life kept you from noticing: you are both mortal and immortal. Your body is the final possession you have to yield. Your spirit is the final possession you get to claim. This is the ultimate faithfulness to the testimony of simplicity.

SEEKING SPIRITUAL CLOSURE

Time is growing short. Your story is moving beyond telling. Now it is more important than ever to figure out the end. What will happen when you die?

In your youth, you had all the time in the world, and you secretly felt immortal. Unless someone crucial to you died, life after death was a hypothetical question; now you are right up against it. Rote answers no longer gloss over it. What can you depend on? Can you count on anything in the end?

You will soon be facing the mystery of death alone. Even if your family and friends are intact, and even if your faith is strong, no one is going with you. Such a solo voyage—like setting out across the Atlantic in a sailboat—calls for courage. But you are no more alone before the All now than you ever were. You are just noticing it better.

Faith and Practice has no explicit statement about the afterlife to reassure you. The Light itself never dies. Bodies fade away; but if there is that of God within you, and God has no beginning or end, could your soul die? For some, this question can be a source of real suffering.

Friends believe in direct experience. A fortunate few have received answers about the afterlife. Some of them have seen radiant light in near-death experiences. Some have seen departed loved ones or heard messages from them. If you are not granted such personal confirmation, these stories might dismay you: "Why doesn't she speak to *me*?" For most people, it is necessary to sit with the question of an afterlife in trust and silence.

For early Quakers, steeped in Christian theology, there was no question. They had touched the living God in worship. They spoke easily of the reward of heaven and life everlasting. Just before he died, James Nayler wrote that he was preparing to leave for the "eternal holy life." William Penn wrote in 1693, "The truest end of life, is to know the Life that never ends."

Some Quakers today hold fast to this belief. Having a sense that there is an afterlife releases them from fear. Marcelle Martin says, "I have increasingly become convinced that our souls remain alive after our bodies die, and that we can touch each other across the gap between this life and the next." Robert Dicken writes, "I am confident about life after death. Although I'm not sure if it is heaven or hell, I am sure of this: since God created this beautiful creation and allowed me to experience it…, I can't believe He would let it evaporate into a dull, dark thud of nothingness at its end."

Many contemporary Friends lean toward other conclusions. Some are drawn to beliefs from another faith. Those who were raised in another religious tradition might fall back on childhood training. One Friend hedged, "I'd better bring the priest back in just in case."

Some prefer to make heaven on earth; others are content with a simple return to nature. Still others say, "My immortality is in the hearts of those who love me."

You are going to find your own way to peace, and silent worship is your ticket. For years, you have had encounters with the Divine— or repeated misses. Perhaps you approached worship wondering, "Does this really work?" and "How am I meant to do this?" Perhaps you said to the Divine, "Show yourself, please," or "Oh, there you are. Here I am," or "What do you want of me now?" Regardless, you kept on practicing. Keep going now.

Spiritual closure takes time; you can't hurry it. Your spirit's struggles toward fullness might take unexpected turns or stop and start. Coincidences and synchronicities will arise; the right person or insight will show up at the right time.

At the end of life, both losing faith and deepening faith are common. Paradoxically, you might experience both at once. Live in the tension. Sometimes, it is only when you are pushed furthest into despair that the walls break down.

God is both in the fullness and in the emptiness. If you face emptiness and loss squarely, if you rest in that difficult suspense, what can emerge is trust in mystery.

Early Friends understood this process as growing into "perfection" or wholeness—an entire faithfulness to the Light. When this happens, it becomes possible to meet yourself in that which is eternal. Then maybe the true word is not "closure," but opening.

STEPPING INTO THE STREAM

Aging and dying need not suddenly overtake you. Indeed, you began training for them from the moment of birth. You left behind the intimate space of the womb and entered a large space; you lost the cord on which you depended, and using unknown lungs, tried breathing on your own. Squalling with surprise, you did it. Every life stage since then has called you—body, mind, and spirit—to let go of something old and move with trust into the unknown.

Douglas Steere reminds us of all the little deaths we have during life—sending a child to school for the first time, the marriage of a daughter, changing your job, and so on. These little deaths are "loosenings" that give us practice for the big death. You can become a person "who for many years has been a companion of death, who has even died again and again, and who in these deaths has had dynamically confirmed... the presence of a Power which is able and eager to sustain...."

You might be practicing for death in an even more powerful way. William Taber describes the experience of dropping into the "Stream of Living Unity." It is just as real for him as stepping into a stream of water. Being in the Stream is what many Friends do in meeting for worship—settling, centering, and shifting together into an alternate consciousness, where Divine Love surrounds them. As they become more practiced, these Friends become certain that they are one with God.

Taber says,

> Like a stream it is always moving, always changing, yet it is still the same stream. We step into the same stream that George Fox entered... the same stream that the apostle Peter knew, the same stream that Mary the mother of Jesus knew, and in some mysterious way, we share with them across twenty centuries of time.

This nonlinear mode, according to Taber, is what the New Testament means by "being in the mind of Christ." Other faiths and practices have their own names for this experience of the highest reality.

Both aging and dying are easier when you stand in this divine stream. Love washes over and around you, buoys you, and connects you to creation. It does not make pain or suffering go away, but it grants a different context for them. Once stepping into the stream becomes second nature, any transformation can feel accompanied and assured—even the final one.

The poet T. S. Eliot says it this way:

We must be still and still moving
Into another intensity,
For a further union, a deeper communion....
In my end is my beginning.

Finding the Voices

Margery Post Abbott, *Walk Humbly, Serve Boldly: Modern Quakers as Everyday Prophets* (San Francisco: Inner Light Books, 2018).

Baltimore Yearly Meeting of the Religious Society of Friends, *2013 Resource for Faith and Practice* (Sandy Spring, MD: Baltimore Yearly Meeting, 2013), "Queries, Advices, and Voices: Aging."

Katy Butler, *The Art of Dying Well: A Practical Guide to a Good End of Life* (New York: Scribner, 2019).

Robert Stephen Dicken, "A Simple State of Being that Never Truly Dies," *Friends Journal* (August 2017). https://www.friendsjournal.org/simple-state-of-being.

T. S. Eliot, "East Coker" (The Four Quartets), *The Complete Poems and Plays 1909–1950* (New York: Harcourt Brace, 1952). Used by permission.

Jenifer Faulkner (1982), as quoted in *Quaker Faith and Practice: The Book of Christian Discipline of the Religious Society of Friends (Quakers) in Britain* (London: Britain Yearly Meeting, 1995), #21.57.

Anne Felton, *One Caregiver's Journey with Dementia*, Pendle Hill Pamphlet 477 (Wallingford, PA: Pendle Hill Publications, 2022).

Margaret Guenther, *Toward Holy Ground: Spiritual Directions for the Second Half of Life* (Boston: Cowley, 1995).

Thích Nhất Hạnh, *Peace Is Every Step: The Path of Mindfulness in Everyday Life* (New York: Bantam Books, 1991).

London Yearly Meeting (1923), as quoted in *Quaker Faith and Practice: The Book of Christian Discipline of the Religious Society of Friends (Quakers) in Britain* (London: Britain Yearly Meeting, 1995), #21.46.

Marcelle Martin, "Between This Life and the Next," *A Whole Heart* (blog), October 17, 2022. https://awholeheart. com/2022/10/17/between-this-life-and-the-next.

Walter Martin (1988), as quoted in *Quaker Faith and Practice: The Book of Christian Discipline of the Religious Society of Friends (Quakers) in Britain* (London: Britain Yearly Meeting, 2013), #21.58.

Mary Morrison, *Gift of Days: Report on an Illness,* Pendle Hill Pamphlet 364 (Wallingford, PA: Pendle Hill Publications, 2003).

James Nayler, "There is a Spirit which I feel" (1660), in *The Works of James Nayler (1618–1660)* (Farmington, ME: Quaker Heritage Press, 2014). http://www.qhpress.org/texts/nayler/thereis.html.

Mary Oliver, "The Summer Day," *New and Selected Poems* (Boston: Beacon, 1992). Used by permission.

Philadelphia Yearly Meeting of the Religious Society of Friends, *Faith and Practice* (Philadelphia: Philadelphia Yearly Meeting, 2017), "Advices III."

Quaker Aging Resources, "End of Life Decision Making and Quaker Testimonies," http://www.quakeragingresources. org/2013/05/end-of-life-decision-making-and-quaker-testimonies.

William Penn (1693), as quoted in *Quaker Faith and Practice: The Book of Christian Discipline of the Religious Society of Friends (Quakers) in Britain* (London: Britain Yearly Meeting, 1995), #22.95.

Richard Rohr and the Center for Action and Contemplation, "Faithful Resilience: The Unitive Way," January 25, 2024, https://cac.org/daily-meditations/the-unitive-way.

May Sarton, "Now I Become Myself," *Collected Poems 1930–1993* (New York: W.W. Norton, 1993).

William Z. Shetter, *Some Thoughts on Becoming Eighty-five*, Pendle Hill Pamphlet 418 (Wallingford, PA: Pendle Hill Publications, 2012).

Bradford Smith, *Dear Gift of Life: A Man's Encounter with Death*, Pendle Hill Pamphlet 142 (Wallingford, PA: Pendle Hill Publications, 1965).

Hannah Whitall Smith (1903), as quoted in *Quaker Faith and Practice: The Book of Christian Discipline of the Religious Society of Friends (Quakers) in Britain* (London: Britain Yearly Meeting, 1995), #21.48.

Dorothy Steere (1995), as quoted in Philadelphia Yearly Meeting of the Religious Society of Friends, *Faith and Practice* (Philadelphia: Philadelphia Yearly Meeting, 2017), "Extracts on Faith Reflected in Practice and Daily Life," #190.

Douglas Steere, *On Beginning from Within* (New York: Harper & Brothers, 1943).

William Taber, *The Mind of Christ: Bill Taber on Meeting for Business*, ed. Michael Birkel, Pendle Hill Pamphlet 406 (Wallingford, PA: Pendle Hill Publications, 2010).

Dylan Thomas, "Do not go gentle into that good night," *The Poems of Dylan Thomas* (New York: New Directions, 1952).

Howard Thurman, as quoted in Bailie Gil, *Violence Unveiled: Humanity at the Crossroads* (New York: Crossroad, 1997).

Elizabeth Watson (1979), as quoted in Philadelphia Yearly Meeting of the Religious Society of Friends, *Faith and Practice* (Philadelphia: Philadelphia Yearly Meeting, 2017), "Extracts on Faith Reflected in Practice and Daily Life," #192.

Charles Williams, from "The Rite of the Passion," in *Three Plays: The Early Metaphysical Plays of Charles Williams* (Oxford: Oxford University Press, 1931).

John Yungblut, *On Hallowing One's Diminishments*, Pendle Hill Pamphlet 292 (Wallingford, PA: Pendle Hill Publications, 1990).

Chapter 2

Reaching the End: Spirit-Led Dying

Dying, then, is not falling off into nothingness, or, worse yet, a failure to live. Rather, it is a beginning, another birth, a return to Largeness.

—Lucy Screechfield McIver, 1998

When you pass through deep waters, I am with you. Walk through fire and you will not be scorched, through flames and they will not burn you.

—Isaiah 43:2, New English Bible

Help me to loosen, fiber by fiber, the instinctive strings that bind me to the life I know. Infuse me with Thy spirit so that it is Thee I turn to, not the old ropes of habit and thought. Make me poised and free, ready when the intimation comes to go forward eagerly and joyfully, into the new phase of life that we call death....

Give me joy in awaiting the great change that comes after this life of many changes; let my self be merged in Thy Self as a candle's wavering light is caught up into the sun.

—Elizabeth Gray Vining, 1978

What I have realized is that "going with grace" is not only something for the moment of death. It starts now in the choices that I make, in my acceptance of death and its nearness and in the way in which I live the remaining time until my dying and death occur.
—Diana Campbell, 2022

If there is any bravery in me, it is in my refusal to let fear eclipse my imagination for anything other than pain. To maintain imagination for both the beautiful *and* the terrible is to marry prudence and hope.
—Cole Arthur Riley, 2024

I don't believe that death comes at the end of life. I believe your death was there at your birth with you. It was the unknown presence. Every step of the road of your life that you take, your death is beside you. Death often works through the vehicle of fear, so as you begin to transfigure your own fear, you are actually transfiguring the presence of your own death.
—John O'Donohue, 2018

Death is no more than a turning of us over from time to eternity. Death then, being the way and condition of life, we cannot love to live, if we cannot bear to die.
—William Penn, 1682

THE END OF YOUR LIFE CALLS for self-love, courage, and honesty. It asks you to step into your power, to be your own best advocate, and to stand by your values all the way. It asks you also to accept your weakness, to be tender with yourself, and to allow others to give you care. It makes you dig deeper than ever for grace and seek the Light in difficult places. This is hard work, but good work.

LIGHTENING YOUR LIFE

A wonderful exercise goes like this: Imagine that you are packing for a far country, and you will be gone forever. Which six possessions do you instantly want to pack? (Size and weight don't matter; this is imaginary. No problem packing a whole farm or a grand piano.) Now, which six people will you choose to accompany you? (Anyone is able to go.) Third, which six qualities that have defined you will you take? (Never mind whether the qualities are "positive" or "negative"; stubbornness and fierceness count as well as humor and kindness.) Now imagine that alas, there is really room for only three of those possessions, people, and qualities. Continue letting go until you discover what is the last to go, the most essential to you.

What are the implications for the way you are living right now? What things, relationships, and ways of being do you want to lay down? To what will you devote yourself from now on? What will you keep to the very last, when everything must go?

This exercise is one way to visualize lightening your spirit as the end draws near. Perhaps, as you grew older, you began setting in order or releasing all you amassed. As the end approaches, this process accelerates. You consider, thank, and lay aside both blessings and burdens.

Ideally, your sense of what you must possess grows ever lighter. Your sense of who you love grows ever clearer. Your sense of who you are grows ever keener. Carrying to the end only what is best and most meaningful, you learn to relax. You are willing to open the way. Death is the far country. You will travel well.

WRITING DOWN YOUR WISHES

"If we want to keep shaping our lives all the way to the end, it helps to imagine, to choose, and to plan," says Katy Butler in *The Art of Dying Well*. You don't know whether your end will be sudden or gradual, early or late—but you do know that you are mortal. It does not help either to harp on this fact or to deny it. It does help to open your spirit to it. Facing your end steadily, you can discover that time is more precious. You can redouble the sweetness of being alive. And you can make ready in specific ways.

Your Advance Directive

If you have not yet created an advance directive, write one today, while you are clearheaded and able. There is no more practical way to live your Quaker values to the end. Carl Magruder, a Quaker hospice chaplain, urges us to talk deliberately about death and dying in our meetings. There is no more useful action you can take to prepare and smooth your way.

An *advance directive* is a set of legal documents regarding your wishes for the end of your life, often combined into one package. An adult in the United States has the right to decide what kinds of medical treatment to allow or refuse. (For a child, tricky issues of guardianship and advocacy can arise.)

Today's remarkable health technology often restores or prolongs life. Do you want to receive any forms of life support—CPR, ventilators, tube feeding, dialysis? Under what circumstances would you want your family to "pull the plug"? For you, what defines being not medically but personally "alive"?

Discern and record what is right for you. Your doctors, partner, and children have their own values and perspectives. So does your culture, which has all kinds of assumptions and prejudices. But no one can make such choices the way you can.

This is not a matter of checking a box; it is a set of questions that deserve nuanced, deeply considered answers. This is an essential way to let your life speak. Your answers will allow your outer life to express your inner life. They are an outgrowth of the testimony of integrity.

An advance directive is a gift to yourself. It is an expression of the testimony of stewardship. You are taking power over your future; you are defining the daunting unknown; you are making yourself capable even when capacity fails. Unexpected events happen at any age; an accident could put you into a sudden coma. In a medical crisis when you are unable to speak, a directive is your voice.

If you are from a social or economic group that has been denied good health care for generations, a directive is an even more essential gift. With the advance directive, you can tell the medical team not to give up on you too soon. Your directive reflects the testimony of equality.

An advance directive is a gift to your family, too. Do not assume they will agree upon the right thing to do when emotional life-and-death decisions are thrust upon them; a medical crisis can tear a family apart. You have a chance to minimize discord and argument, in accordance with the testimony of peace. In the most extreme case, if the family is divided, decisions can end up in court. There your written voice could make all the difference.

Guiding the family's thinking, your directive also relieves them from second-guessing, guilt, and regret for years to come. It pulls them together and frees them to share mourning at a time when solidarity is sorely needed. In this way you guide them in the testimony of community.

Finally, an advance directive is a gift to your medical care team. Without it, they can wind up in a hard position: they are legally required to do everything possible to keep you alive, even against your wishes and their own best judgment.

You have the right to change your mind at any point, and dying people often do. But when all parties are aware of an advance directive, it can have a strong influence on your care. It simplifies a fraught situation, in accord with the testimony of simplicity. Indeed, hospitals ask all patients whether they have a directive and provide a form if they do not. For everyone's sake, complete an advance directive.

From state to state, advance directives vary, but they have many similarities. They all require two witnesses, neither of whom can be your named health care agent. West Virginia is the only state in Baltimore Yearly Meeting that requires notarization. Some documents are recognized in all states, some only in the state you live in. If you move to another state or spend a lot of time there, check that state's rules to be sure that your advance directive remains valid.

Advance directives do *not* require a lawyer. You can get them online from your state government's website, at your doctor's office, at a senior center, or at the nearest hospital. If you live in Virginia, see https://honoringchoices-va.org. Honoring Choices will help you complete an advance medical directive in person without charge. "Five Wishes," an easily understood variant of an advance directive, is accepted in most states, including all four states and Washington, DC in Baltimore Yearly Meeting. It is available in thirty languages and in Braille. You can get it for a small fee from https://agingwithdignity.org.

Another option is http://mydirectives.com, a commercial website that stores directives in digital form. The company charges medical providers for its service; the service is free to you but it does use your data (without identifying you) for profit. If you are traveling in the mid-Atlantic region, this option allows many hospitals to find your directives.

Using any of these websites, you can print out directives for family and friends, medical providers, and hospitals. If your doctor's practice has a patient portal, you can upload your directive to it.

Your Medical Power of Attorney

Advance directives typically have two parts. The first part is a *medical power of attorney*. You designate a person (sometimes called a health care agent or proxy) to be your voice. You give the person HIPAA clearance to see all your medical records. This is the person you trust to make medical decisions when you cannot advocate for yourself.

Selecting this person is a serious decision that should neither be rushed nor delayed. Choose someone who understands your basic beliefs and values, honors them, and will use them to resolve unexpected issues.

Ask the person's permission to be so named. It is important to have deep conversations with your agent about what you want. Talk about your beliefs, your values, and how you make hard decisions in ambiguous situations.

You need a person who is careful but decisive. A good agent is levelheaded, reliable, and available. It is ideal for the agent to live near enough to make decisions at your bedside. Your agent must be diplomatic and calmly assertive with loved ones. The agent must tell your story well, communicate your values, and persevere in advocating for you to all care providers, throughout the complexity of the health care system.

Your agent need not be a family member or even your primary caregiver. Narrow the choice to just one person. If you wish, you can encourage your agent to seek input from others. It is a kindness to tell the family who your agent is, rather than letting them discover your choice during a crisis. This is part of maintaining peace and community.

Legally, the agent must be at least eighteen years old and cannot own, operate, or work at a health facility where you live. It is wise to designate a backup agent, or even to make a prioritized list of backups.

If you have no medical power of attorney and you cannot make decisions, you have a legal crisis on top of a medical crisis. State law will designate a health care agent, usually in order of spouse, parent, child, and sibling. Assigning a legal guardian for "unbe-friended" patients can be a costly process, taking weeks or months. Meanwhile, life-sustaining measures continue, even if that is not what you would have desired.

Your Living Will

The second part of an advance directive in some states is called a *living will*. It deals with treatment in three extreme situations:

1. When you suddenly need life support to prevent imminent death. Examples are cardiac arrest, respiratory arrest, some aneurysms, and some gunshot wounds.
2. When you are in a persistent vegetative state; that is, when you are deemed permanently unconscious. This designation is made after thirty days in a coma.
3. When you reach the end stage of an advanced, incurable disease such as Alzheimer's or when you are in major organ failure.

For each of these situations, you choose one of three ways to be treated.

The first choice is "Keep me comfortable and allow natural death to occur." This choice asks for comfort care instead of extending your life with medical interventions. It means "no poking and prodding" and no life support. This choice triggers a Do Not Resuscitate (DNR) order. It is also called a Comfort Only order.

The second choice still includes a DNR, but it allows artificial nutrition and hydration. This choice means you want to get food and water by intravenous drip or a feeding tube. This middle ground honors certain personal, cultural, and religious preferences.

The third choice is "Try to extend my life for as long as possible." This choice asks for all possible treatment. Even so, doctors do not have to provide treatment that is "medically futile." Maryland is one of the few states where doctors are legally protected for withholding treatment that is "ethically indefensible," doing more harm than good.

What if your condition does not fit neatly into one of these three boxes? You can say in your living will that you want your agent to follow either the letter of your directive or the spirit of it.

There is a space in the living will in which to state your goals and values. One Friend wanted care "so long as I am able to laugh and enjoy beauty." One asked to withhold care "if I am not likely to recover to communicate and to live without constant expert attendance." Another wrote that she did not want to be on life support "unless it is a bridge to wellness."

In this space, you might detail your preferences for pain relief. You could request different treatment under special circumstances. For example, some Friends state, "If I am pregnant, keep me alive so long as the baby is viable." Some Friends say, "If I have advanced dementia, do not keep me on life support." Your dear ones will welcome the clear articulation of your wishes.

This is also the place to tell what you want to have happen after you die. You can record intentions for organ donation, funeral arrangements, and burial. To help you choose what happens to your body, read "Gifting Your Body" in Chapter 3 and "Considerations for Laying Your Body Down" in the Treasury of Resources.

Medical and Physician Orders

Much stronger instruments than an advance directive, *medical and physician orders* are created in a different way. You tell your wishes to a doctor, physician assistant, or nurse practitioner, who signs a form.

Unlike an advance directive, this form is not a record of wishes. It is a medical order that is legally binding in all medical settings—inpatient, outpatient, in an ambulance, or at home.

If you are fairly healthy, an advance directive is sufficient. Medical orders are intended for "medically fragile" people with such serious illness that doctors would not be surprised if they died within a year. When EMTs take you from the hospital to another facility, this order directs them to give either life support or comfort care along the way. If they pick you up at home, they check for such an order on your refrigerator door.

Medical orders have different names in each state: MOLST (Medical Orders for Life-Sustaining Treatment) in Maryland, POLST (Pennsylvania Orders for Life-Sustaining Treatment) in Pennsylvania, POST (Physician Orders for Scope of Treatment) in Virginia, and MOST (Medical Orders for Scope of Treatment) in the District of Columbia and West Virginia.

If you do not want resuscitation of your heart and lungs, have your doctor sign a Do Not Resuscitate (DNR) order. Then carry a DNR card in your wallet or wear a medical necklace or bracelet. Typically, this jewelry must be engraved with the name and phone number of the doctor who wrote the order. In the crucial moments of deciding whether or not to perform CPR, EMTs look for these signals. Lacking them, you will get CPR, no matter what.

COMMUNICATING YOUR WISHES

Writing down your wishes is only the first step. These documents do you no good if no one knows about them.

Talk with your doctors and your health care agent to make sure they understand what is important to you. In serious illness, the workbook *What Matters to Me* (https://theconversationproject.org) will help prepare you to talk with your medical team. Give copies of your advance directive to your agent and your alternate agent. Keep them on file with your doctors and at the nearest hospital. Whenever you are admitted to a hospital, bring them to the attention of the hospital's medical team.

An additional means of communicating these wishes is a Vial of Life. Kept on or in your refrigerator or your car's glove box, this packet summarizes your medical condition and has room for your advance directive. You post a decal on your refrigerator and your front door to alert EMTs.

These documents are great jumping-off points for a conversation with your loved ones about end of life. You will be doing more than securing your own needs. This is a teaching moment, in which you can help dear ones come to peace with losing you someday. "Because I love you," one Friend began, "I want to make you comfortable ahead of time. You can ask me anything about this." Thus she opened a tender mutual sharing.

At any age, but especially if they are younger, people often shy away from this conversation, which sparks anticipatory grief and denial. Look around for someone who is receptive. A Friend says, "My sons refused to discuss it, so I went to my daughter-in-law, and she broke the ice." "Never be afraid of talking about your dying wishes," said Frances Taber in her early nineties. "You can't talk enough about them."

Be persistent; you can find conversation starters at https://theconversationproject.org. You will likely rest easier when at least someone in your family has heard your wishes. Keep following through. Susan Johns Smith writes, "My father died at ninety-two years old. Although he had advance directives, the most powerful thing he did at the end of his life was to begin saying *No*."

In the hospital, good communication with your health care agent and with your family will make them better advocates for you. Hospitalists—physicians employed to oversee care in the hospital—will not know you and might not share your values. They change from shift to shift, and old medical orders can get overlooked. Each new set of caregivers will need to get up to speed on what is important to you. Having an engaged advocate by your bedside is the best protection for your wishes.

Renew the conversation with yourself at regular intervals. As your spirit keeps growing, you do not want to be bound by outdated decisions. You can change any part of an advance directive, including your agent, at any time, as long as you are still able to make decisions. You can tailor your wishes to conditions likely to arise with a new diagnosis. (See "Readings and Support" in the Treasury of Resources for forms specific to dementia.) It is generally advised that you reexamine your health care wishes at least every ten years up to the time you are sixty, and then every five years thereafter. Another rule of thumb for when to review is the "five Ds":

- the start of a new Decade
- the Death of your health care agent
- a Divorce, if your health care agent is your former spouse
- a change of Diagnosis
- a marked Decline in health

Once you update any part of your advance directive, destroy all copies of the previous version, so no one will be confused or mistaken. Tell loved ones and your agent about changes. Inform your doctor and ask for any appropriate change in medical orders. Then as need arises, your voice will shine through.

FACING UP TO CHANGE

Physical and mental changes can arise dramatically or so subtly you barely notice. You might be the first to notice a change in your health, whether in mind or body. You begin to question or distrust yourself. Don't dismiss this discovery, but don't let fear run away with you, either. Just acknowledge it and pay attention. Share your symptoms with a trusted friend for a more objective view. Is it worth pursuing? Do you need a medical assessment?

Perhaps someone else points out a change in you. Treat this observation as a gift, and do not brush it aside. Take it seriously, neither exaggerating nor downplaying your own sense of your condition. You know yourself best, but someone else can open your eyes.

How serious is the change? Life-threatening conditions like uncontrolled bleeding, head trauma, or chest pain need instant emergency care. A new lump or a blackout or an unexplained weight loss call for attention in the near future. On the other hand, there are irritating impairments you can live with, such as mild arthritis or subtle hearing loss. Perhaps you put on a knee brace, take vitamins, take naps, get a massage, or pray for endurance. But once any change begins to interfere with your function or enjoyment, you need medical care.

Do not wait for change to knock you off your feet. Long before then, develop a relationship with a doctor you trust. Find one who is experienced with issues of aging and willing to discuss them. Choose a doctor who listens to you well.

Go ahead and make an appointment. There are a lot of reasons why people resist going to see a doctor—cost, fear, appearing weak, or losing independence. But the testimony of stewardship is a good guide here. You are making use of the doctor's expertise to take charge of your life.

Before you go to the doctor, make a list of your questions. It's hard to think of everything on the spot, appointments can be short, and a medical context can feel intimidating. Also make a list of symptoms. Details are good—for instance, dates, duration, circumstances, and severity. Continuing to keep such notes will bring patterns to light, allow you clarity, and give your doctor insight.

If there is a chance that this issue is serious, don't go alone. Choose somebody dear to go with you, someone with a comfortable calm presence, to help you listen well and process what you hear. This person should not make choices for you but take notes and verify that you have heard what the doctor says, fully and correctly. You deserve someone who stays by your side through visits, tests, and treatments.

Center yourself before the appointment. Approach it with the same calm, open spirit you bring to meeting for worship. You go to meeting willing to transform, no matter whether you receive a message of challenge or reassurance. One Friend speaks the Serenity Prayer. Another says, "In the waiting room, I silently ask a blessing upon myself and upon the doctor."

GETTING A SERIOUS DIAGNOSIS

A serious diagnosis rocks the ground under you. "The message now comes home," Bradford Smith writes in *Dear Gift of Life*, "strange and yet familiar: I too am mortal." Perhaps at first you feel helpless. Commonly there is shock and disbelief.

John Youngblut writes in *On Hallowing One's Diminishments*,

When I first learned the nature of this illness... and the inescapable prognosis, I went through an inwardly staged protest movement for a time. Denial, disbelief: "It will go away." Then anger, rebellion, challenge: "Why me?" followed by self-pity and incredulity. I was threatened by despair and depression when I thought of the negative effect it would have on my vocation.

But another Friend recounts, "After I heard the news, I went out into the garden and prayed. And I heard the words, 'You are loved, you are not alone, and it will be okay.' These words became a mantra for the rest of my life." That guidance helped her take her diagnosis as a new beginning, a new stage of being.

You can do the same. You have managed new beginnings before—a new home, a new job, a new marriage. Now you are going to make choices that best honor your body and soul.

Gather your spirit and empower yourself by asking plenty of questions. Participate in planning for your own care. Use the doctor as a wise instrument for healing, but don't surrender your voice or your decision-making power.

Ask first: Is this diagnosis definite? Should I wait and retest? Should I get clarifying tests or a second opinion?

Then come questions about treatment: What treatment is being recommended, and why? Is it a cure, or does it simply buy time? What are my odds? Is there an alternative treatment? What are the side effects of each treatment, and will they change how I function?

If this is a life-threatening diagnosis, ask, "How much time do I have *with* treatment?" Also ask, "How much time do I have *without* treatment? What would I experience?" Ask how much time you have to make this decision. You have a lot to take in and a lot at stake.

What will treatment cost, and do any programs offer financial assistance? Who will coordinate the care? Would integrative medicine modalities such as acupuncture and homeopathy make the course of treatment easier? Sometimes the answers are hard, sometimes reassuring—and sometimes there are no answers.

It is likely you will discover follow-up questions. In that event, go back to the doctor for another conversation. Take time for learning, prayer, and reflection. Hold your choice in the Light until you reach clarity.

Realize that any prognosis is tricky, because it is a generalization. No one knows the whole of your particular story. You are not a statistic. Some people are less resilient; others break the pattern and survive.

Remember always that you have spiritual resources to draw upon. Many Friends have shared that a terminal diagnosis opened the way to a spiritual world they had not known existed. Though it was indeed a shaky time with many diagnostic tests, doctor visits, and coordination of schedules and helpers, it was also a time of deepening. Some speak of being enfolded in the loving arms of the Divine. Some speak of spirit guides, saints, or angels. Pushing the door open into that dimension required a crisis and a leap of faith.

DECIDING ABOUT TREATMENT

"After my diagnosis," says one Friend, "there were many voices inside me, all shouting at once and disagreeing." Among the contradictory voices you might hear are the will to live at all costs and the urge not to suffer; the desire to help dear ones grow and the need to protect them from prolonged distress; the hope of fulfilling long-standing dreams and the attraction of a quiet and easy end. There is fear of living a diminished life and optimism that you can live with love and purpose no matter what.

Outside you there are more voices. Medical personnel, trained to value life above all, are urging you to let them act. Not all doctors will agree about the course of treatment. Your cultural training is telling you how to feel about living with different functionality. Each family member has an opinion, whether spoken aloud, internalized, or imagined. All the voices pull you to decide their way.

One Friend who experienced this tumult shares, "I realized I had a familiar process to handle it. I imagined inviting all my voices to sit down together in a meeting for worship. They waited quietly and gently. No voice drowned out another, and gradually I let the sense of the meeting arise. At last, a greater Voice made itself heard."

Another Friend relates, "Part of my process in deciding about treatment was to ask Spirit for guidance. I got a lot of insight in the form of dreams. The other thing I did was to negotiate with God. I said, 'If you want me to do this, give me help—with my children, my endurance, my sleep, and my pain.' I asked the Light to transmute my fear into Love, and to send any unhelpful fear away. And help absolutely came."

Accepting the reality of a diagnosis can make choosing easier. As one person puts it, "I am a Quaker, and I am not at war with cancer. The choice is not about *fighting*. Instead, I am going to trust that the situation is God's will for me, and any course I choose will be an instrument of Love."

The testimony of integrity is invaluable now. Who are you at your core, and which action will help you stand fast in that truth, faithful to your values? How can you best live out your time? How can you thrive amid your new circumstances?

Values, and the goals that embody them, keep you vibrant. They are the reasons you seek health care in the first place. They also can guide your choice to embrace treatment or not. Choosing treatment, one Friend described her goal: "Family is my soul's center. Yes, whatever it takes, I must live to see my granddaughter get married." Another affirmed, "I am above all still an explorer. Help me live to stand on the Great Wall of China." Yet another determined, "My work as peacemaker is not yet complete. I want to make peace in my family, and I won't let pain stop me." On the other hand is the Friend who declared, "For ninety-four years, I have been grateful for a simple life. That is who I am. I choose no fuss and no drawn-out treatment."

The Quaker testimony of stewardship is yet another guide. It asks you to care rightly for your body, your resources, and your time on earth. Would a long course of chemotherapy or an extensive surgery mean good stewardship to you? Some people assert, "Yes, certainly! I have so much to live for. Give me every chance I have. If there is 90 percent mortality, I mean to be in the other 10 percent."

Others respond simply, "I know it is my time to go." Over and over, a Friend who was a nurse saw the toll that treatment could take on quality of life. Confronted with pancreatic cancer of her own, she chose "going with grace." She wrote, "The strength that comes from inner listening is giving me hope and peace."

Unless your end is fast, this kind of choice—to treat or not, to treat aggressively or conservatively—will arise more than once. Expect a series of choices. As your condition changes, there will be fresh decisions. Sometimes new treatments or new drugs will be approved if you hang on. With some treatments, like a double mastectomy, there is no turning back; but with regimens like chemotherapy, you always have a chance to stop.

Just do not second-guess yourself. At each point, affirm whatever choice you make with your whole heart and soul.

Your perspective now is different from when you were younger. Your sense of what is right to do will continue to shift, reflecting your overall health, your hopes for the future, and the importance you place on quality of life. From a Quaker perspective, there is no fixed right or wrong. You need only be true to yourself and to the Light within.

Pastoral care is important when deciding about treatment. One cancer patient says, "I felt like I was lost in a storm in the middle of the ocean. Then my friend offered to create a committee of support.

They agreed to walk beside me through all my choices. She had thrown me a lifeline."

Keep holding your situation in the Light and asking others to hold you. That way your choices will be born of wisdom and love, not desperation or panic. Surround yourself with people who support you while you choose and then uphold the choices you make, practically and emotionally. Have tender patience with those who cannot do so.

EASING TERMINAL PAIN

Most people are not afraid of death itself but of physical pain along the way. They assume that every step toward dying means an increase of pain.

In fact, with a terminal condition, there is *not* always pain. Some end-stage diseases are painless, although if you have preexisting chronic pain, it will persist. Provided mitigation begins soon enough, there are ways to address even potentially severe pain. For example, if you begin early, pain can be managed in many cancers. Hospice succeeds in managing physical suffering for almost all its patients.

Pain has many faces. Sometimes it is a protective alarm; it reminds you to respect your limits or to get help. It tells you that the fall fractured your hip or that your medication is eroding your gut lining. It tells you to put down the heavy milk jug or to treat the bladder infection before it damages your kidneys. Pain tells you to pay attention before your energy is sapped. For this reason, people who get pain relief often live longer.

Pain almost always has an emotional dimension. Some people interpret pain as punishment for something they did. Some feel ashamed to admit they cannot tolerate pain. Untreated pain provokes tension and anxiety, which make it worse in turn. Today's pain can trigger old memories and fears that compound discomfort at the end of life.

When fear magnifies pain, it is time to explore your fear. Is there real danger, or can you reassure yourself? Are stressors intensifying pain, and can you remove them? You might want to seek out counseling. You might ask for a spiritual friend or a support committee. You might petition Spirit for relief. For some people prayer softens fear; praying reminds them who they are apart from pain. Prayer eased one Friend dying of cancer until she described herself as only "*comfortably* afraid."

Your family and culture likely have prejudices about pain control. One Friend says, "My parents told me to be tough, not a weakling or a crybaby." Another notes the opposite: "My family reached for medication at the first twinge." Perhaps it was drilled into you that "It's all in your head," or "God never gives us more than we can bear," or "Faith will provide everything you need."

Nothing in Quaker practice makes a virtue of hurting. Set aside such paradigms and let your spirit discern what is true for you.

Do not take pain for granted or underestimate it. In the context of aging, we often accept as natural that "my old bones creak." We take wear and tear as part of life and laugh that it beats the alternative. But end of life pain is something else, stealing the time your spirit needs to prepare and transform.

There are three basic rules of pain management:

1. *Pain is what you say it is* and not what the medical provider thinks it ought to be. Maybe you have a high pain threshold and do not flinch at much, or maybe you feel every tiny movement as a challenge. Make sure the prescriber is personalizing pain management for your own experience.
2. *The right dose of pain medication reduces pain to a level that you can live with.* Listen to your body and insist that the doctor listens to you. A responsible doctor will start low and go slow, but you will know when the dose is finally right.
3. *Catch pain early.* This is easier and safer than chasing pain once it gets out of control.

To be heard well, you have to describe pain well. Where is it exactly? Is it always there, and how long has it been there? Does it radiate to other parts of your body? Is it a dull ache? Is it a stabbing, shooting, burning, tingling, or stinging pain? Does anything make it better or worse—medications, exercise, heat, massage? Does it wake you up? Does it interfere with work, daily activities, appetite, or relationships? And how bad is it on a scale from 0 (no pain) to 10 (the worst pain ever)? Write down the answers. They are crucial to a good medical assessment. They will help you get the right treatment.

Be relentless in advocacy for yourself. If you can't do that, bring someone with you who will push for answers. Is there a pain clinic? Are other specialists available? Would physical or occupational therapy help? How about acupuncture or myofascial release or cannabis? Are there research trials that deal with your issue? Should you ask for palliative care?

When you are in terminal pain and under professional care, opioids have a legitimate role. In this case, drugs are not killing you—the disease is. Do not worry about addiction. There usually is not enough time to create psychological dependence, and physical side effects can be controlled. Talk to your doctor about how awake and aware you want to remain. Your medical team should show you how to store medications securely so no one can steal or misuse them.

Even in pain, you can always turn to Spirit. Indeed, sometimes you turn because of pain, not in spite of it. One Friend shares:

> I find consolation in the fact that Jesus too suffered and died. His passion reminds me that I am not alone and that what my ordeal is could be much worse.... In fact, the reality of Jesus's passion draws me into a sense of solidarity with others who are suffering.

Choosing Palliative Care

To minimize suffering and maximize comfort, you can turn in several directions for care. All of them can be grounded in Love.

Palliative care is an interdisciplinary medical service that focuses on your quality of life—to help you live on your own terms, as well as possible, for as long as you can. It advocates for you at any stage of a life-threatening disease. It is not as well-known as hospice, but it is increasingly available. It is appropriate for any patient of any age. If you are hospitalized with a serious diagnosis, you can request that a palliative care provider partner with your medical team.

Palliative care practitioners pay close attention to you as a whole person—not just as a patient. They ask, "What is most important to you now?" If you want above all to be pain-free for your daughter's wedding or to have enough energy to finish writing your book, they will intercede with your doctors to help make it happen if at all possible.

An unusual benefit is that a palliative-care team has more time to sit down and listen. It allows them to discern what is really happening to you. They notice how you are eating, sleeping, moving, and coping. Palliative care staff are often connected to lawyers, social workers, home health services, nutritionists, and chaplains who respond quickly to referrals. This close and personalized attention opens the way for you to focus your energies on living and loving. They free you up for the spiritual work that is yours to do.

Unlike hospice, palliative care lets you receive chemotherapy, surgery, or radiation. Palliative care specialists manage pain and watch for side effects of medications other doctors are prescribing. They help you think through the big picture to create or update advance directives. Knowing your specific disease trajectory, they explain what issues you might face and what life-support treatments might be of benefit.

Most hospitals offer this service to their patients, but you might have to ask for it. Medicare and most insurance plans cover it.

Outside the hospital, community-based palliative care takes on patients before they qualify for hospice. Unfortunately, there are not enough such providers. See https://getpalliativecare.org for a current listing of services near you.

CHOOSING HOSPICE

The most familiar choice of end of life care is *hospice*. Hospice offers comfort, dignity, and care all the way to the end. You are eligible if you meet two conditions. First, there is no longer hope for a cure or you have decided to refuse treatment. Second, two physicians certify that, if the disease follows its usual course, you are likely to have less than six months to live.

Dementia alone does not qualify someone for hospice. The course of dementia takes an average of ten years from discovery to death, and hospice in the United States comes in only at the last stage.

Hospice comes to serve you wherever you are. If you are at home and need equipment such as a hospital bed, oxygen, or a wheelchair, hospice will bring it to you. They might even help you move furniture to set up the space for care. If you are in a nursing home, the hospice team will work with the staff.

Typically, hospice is a service, but not a place. However, some hospices do have an inpatient care center. Such a facility provides temporary respite for a caregiver, handles a crisis, or cares for a patient in the last few days of life.

Hospice brings in a team. Nurses focus on pain relief and symptom management. They do regular assessments, medication review, wound care, and family education. Nursing aides help with bathing and dressing. Social workers help you and your family with social, financial, and emotional support. Chaplains tend to your spiritual needs. A physical or occupational therapist might be called in briefly. There might be a Reiki practitioner, a music therapist, or a pet therapist. Volunteers might sit with you, read aloud, or prepare a meal.

Another part of the comfort is that you need not worry about cost. Hospice works with whatever coverage you have. Medicare Part B covers comfort medications, supplies, and the work of the whole team. Medicare Advantage, Medicaid, and most other insurance providers will bill Part B. If necessary, most hospices donate care.

What is not included? In hospice you cannot have any treatment that attempts to cure. You have turned from cure to comfort. You cannot have life-support interventions such as blood transfusions, IVs, or dialysis. You can have tube feeding and take vitamins, but at your own expense. Hospice does not pay for room and board at a nursing home or for full-time aides at home. Ambulance fees and hospitalization for any reason are not covered. For example, if you fall and break your hip, you have to revoke hospice to get surgery and be readmitted to hospice once the hospital releases you.

If you are in hospice, you need a Do Not Resuscitate order. This does not mean you will be abandoned. It does mean that when your heartbeat or breathing ceases, you will be allowed to die naturally, surrounded by tender care.

You might have several hospices among which to choose. Choose one with an impeccable reputation. Notice whether there is an inpatient facility. Ask how many hours their aides can help you, what other services are available, and whether they have volunteers. Some hospices are for-profit, some are not, and sometimes the difference in services is surprising.

There is a myth that you die as soon as you get into hospice. The truth is that many people delay enrollment until they are nearly dead. Would you and your doctor be surprised to find you alive in six months, regardless of treatment? If the answer is yes, then it is appropriate to explore the option. Commonly, hospice patients and their families say they only regret not having entered sooner.

In fact, entering hospice does not even mean that you will die soon. You are free to choose to leave for curative treatment or a clinical trial. Hospice provides such a comprehensive safety net that nearly 15 percent of patients become so stable they no longer qualify.

Choosing to Stop

The medical establishment is trained to treat you and will tend to keep recommending interventions to the end, even when those interventions just prolong dying.

It is possible, however, to take your ending into your own hands. Such choices ought never to be made on impulse, but only after deep discernment. Because they are controversial, this is a place where the testimony of community is vital.

Talk it over with close loved ones and members of your community. You owe it to them, because choosing this kind of death will have a deep effect upon many more people than you might suppose, and the effects can linger for years.

Ask for a clearness committee to test your decision. (See "Queries for Discerning a Leading to Die" in the Treasury of Resources.) Is it a true leading? Briefly, a clearness committee is composed of a few close and deeply grounded individuals who help you clarify what you are considering. Listening deeply, they will help you explore every ramification of your situation—physical, emotional, and spiritual. Maybe the problem is that you lack an advocate, or your pain is not being addressed, or you need help with depression. Maybe you really are called to stop. In the committee's presence you can arrive at your highest and best course of action.

If you choose one of the endings described below, be sure spiritual supporters stay with you throughout the process and help you follow through. Also be sure to record your intention in an advance directive or another witnessed document, so there can be no later allegations of elder abuse or murder. Be aware that after a certain point, you will be unable to change your mind.

No Medical Interventions

One option is to allow nature to take its course without medical intervention. It is your legal right to make this choice. For example, one Friend who was 102 years old decided not to replace the battery on her pacemaker. Another Friend, fiercely independent, chose not to call 911 when she had a heart attack. A third Friend in her mid-nineties obtained a doctor's order not to admit her to the hospital for any reason.

Some Friends decide it is a waste of resources even to do routine diagnostic tests at a certain age, such as tests for thyroid hormone or cholesterol level. This is their interpretation of the testimonies of stewardship and integrity.

Another Friend tells the story of her father's death. He had told his family emphatically to allow no intervention: "I am waiting for the bus to heaven, to join your mother." At ninety-four, suffering congestive heart failure, he contracted pneumonia. At this point, the family did not send him to the hospital for IV antibiotics. "We are honoring his wishes," they said. "Pneumonia is his ticket on the bus to heaven."

Voluntarily Stopping Eating and Drinking

Another option is Voluntarily Stopping Eating and Drinking (VSED). Even when you do not make this choice, knowing it is possible can give you a comforting sense of agency.

Fasting until you die is your legal right, unless you are in prison or a mental hospital. Nursing homes are legally required to offer food but cannot make you eat it.

The process of VSED typically takes seven to ten days; for younger people, it can last longer. Abstaining from food but accepting water can add weeks. Hunger and thirst gradually diminish; the stomach shrinks and the gut slows down. Fasting does not hurt.

Hospice is a valuable ally here. They can ease the pain of your underlying condition. They can calm confusion, interpret what is happening, and support your family. Surround yourself also with people whose tender assurance will keep you steadfast. These helpers in turn will benefit from the support of your Quaker meeting.

Well-known Friends have used VSED, including Kenneth Boulding and Scott Nearing. Within Baltimore Yearly Meeting in recent years, there have been several instances. One Friend in her nineties with stomach cancer decided to stop eating and faded away. Another Friend, with a progressive neurological disease, initiated a fast when she began to need a feeding tube, with the full agreement of her support committee. A third Friend had a stroke that left her suddenly unable to swallow. She too chose VSED. These testimonies left a lasting impact on the Friends House Retirement Community in Sandy Spring, Maryland.

Lucy McIver speaks of a Friend with end-stage Parkinson's who chose to dedicate his fast to global hunger. He used fasting to draw attention to the hungry and to unite with them. "He came to feel inwardly that his suffering somehow lessened the pain of others who had no food." For him, this connection gave the end of his life meaning.

A modified version of VSED is a way to help someone with dementia who has previously expressed a steadfast desire not to linger. The guideline is "Don't offer, don't refuse." One Friend and her sisters gathered to tend their mother as her death drew close. They stopped reminding her to eat or drink and just provided a little something when she asked. As the family helped one another keep compassionate vigil, their mother gently tapered her intake to nothing and died.

Medical Aid in Dying

A third option is Medical Aid in Dying (MAID). In this case you ask a specially certified physician to write you a prescription for a lethal mix of drugs, which you take by yourself. This process is not the same as euthanasia, in which others administer medication.

Where MAID is legal, many safeguards are in place. You must be an adult. Two doctors must certify that you are terminally ill, have six months or less to live, and have full decision-making capacity. You must be able to put the drugs into your own mouth. Two doctors and two independent witnesses must confirm that no coercion exists. Some states have even more stipulations. MAID was legal in eleven jurisdictions as of 2023, while some states actively prohibited it.

Though you take the drugs by yourself, you need not be alone; you can be in the company of those willing to support you. You will need a clear advance directive to protect them. Be aware that it might take many long, hard conversations to bring them to agree. Also know that this choice still could be a grievous blow to people you know.

Proponents of MAID speak of autonomy and dignity. They say that having the option relieves their fear and anxiety. Many patients who request prescriptions never fill them, and of those, far fewer use them. Most people who follow through are white, college-educated patients with incurable degenerative diseases.

Quakers are deeply divided on this issue. Leeds Area Meeting in England wrestled with it in a book, *Assisted Dying: A Quaker Exploration*. Homewood Monthly Meeting wrote a minute supporting legislation for MAID in Maryland in 2019. There are Friends around the world who are actively supporting MAID.

On the other hand, many Friends oppose MAID on the grounds of the sanctity of life. They point out that your life is not yours alone. Many chaplains say that this option removes time at the end for making peace and letting the Divine work in unforeseen ways. Parents of disabled children fear that this precedent will be misused. Others object that if palliative care were more widely available, fewer people would seek this option.

Let your Quaker values guide you. Any one of these choices might open smoothly before you or require a struggle. Quaker theologian Benjamin J. Wood writes, "Our plea as disquieted Friends should be simply this: Whatever you feel is right, lay it before God and your meeting, and test your discernment."

EXPERIENCING THE END

What is it like to die? Your experience will be as unique as your life is. What your caregiver, family, or friends observe might not match your own inner experience.

Physically, except in a sudden death, bodies go through a typical pattern as life fades. A spiritual shift seems to accompany each physical shift. Knowing these stages might relax your fears. If you have some idea what to expect, if you know that this is a natural progression, you are less likely to panic. Knowledge is comforting and calming. You are not alone, but laboring within the community of those who have died before you.

Months before passing, your energy diminishes and you sleep more. It can be a time of vivid dreams. You are less hungry and thirsty. You might need help with toileting and grooming. You might ache from moving less. You are likely to withdraw from people and activities. This retreat often gets labeled as depression, but it can also be a sign of physical discomfort or of a spiritual turn inward.

Weeks before passing, you are too tired to get out of bed without help. Your sense of time shifts, so you might sleep through the day and wake through the night. Your sense of taste is apt to change, too, and favorite foods might become unappealing. It gets hard to swallow anything, including medicine. With less nourishment, skin becomes fragile. You sometimes appear disoriented, confused, or delirious.

Days before passing, you are usually bedbound, and you have to be repositioned to prevent pressure sores. You need help with all care. You are not likely to want food or water, and the output of urine decreases. You might murmur to people others cannot see, reach into the air, or pick at the covers. You seem to be sleeping all the time. Perhaps all your consciousness is focused on taking the next breath. Perhaps you are intent on waking into another mode of being. No one knows but you.

Hours before passing, every physical system is letting go. There are pauses in breathing. Circulation slows, and the skin becomes cool, mottled, and blue. Blood pressure drops. There might be incontinence. Accumulated saliva causes a rattle in the throat. You might seem restless. Bursts of energy or clarity can allow moments of almost normal communication; these are final gifts to the people around you.

At death, your body simply relaxes. Often Friends who have kept vigil report a sense of freshness, sweetness, and even exaltation at the time of death. One Friend recalls, "When my husband died, the room filled up with light." Though there is a moment when death is officially certified, many witnesses attest that the liberation of spirit can be either swift or gradual.

The spiritual side of this story is not easy to interpret from outside. Is delirium an organic breakdown, as a doctor might explain, or a true spiritual communication—or both? Often a dying person speaks to someone who is not physically present or who has already died. Is this a true encounter? Language of departure is common: "I want to go home," "I need to pack my bags," or "I have to catch the train." Is this the plain perception of an unfolding journey?

Love or loose ends will hold some people back. A great many people wait to die until those they love give permission or assurance that survivors will be all right. Other people hesitate to reach the point of surrender. At that point, they let go swiftly.

Still others linger in a liminal space. It is as if the spirit is under-going a long reverse labor, dying toward a new birth into a sacred space. One Friend tells this story about her mother's death: "My mother asked me, 'Why is this taking so long? Where am I? Have I died yet?' I told her she was probably coming and going. Noticeably comforted, she said, 'Yes, that's right,' and fell back into a deep peaceful sleep."

Marcelle Martin reports that a dying Friend

> had several experiences of entering into heaven: moments when the heaviness of his body in his hospital bed faded, and he felt he entered into a realm of pure love, infused with light. He was joyfully welcomed by his father, who had died many years before, and also by his grandfather, whom he had never met. He also felt himself being embraced from behind by God, as though he were sitting on God's lap.

"Heaven is right here but in a different dimension," Jim told me.

Friends who come back from a near-death experience have reported moving into a great Light, a sense of peace, and a merging into vast, unconditional love. One Friend says that this experience made her no longer afraid of being dead:

> I saw death not as non-being but as a further form of being. I had a new understanding of those who do not fight a terminal diagnosis. I want to reach for that same unconditional love here and now, in this lifetime.

A TIME OF MINISTRY

Ideally, when all the motions of the spirit find completion, a dying person reunites with the Divine. When this happens, it is an oppor-tunity for extraordinary ministry.

On the one hand, Spirit can move those who witness a death. A Quaker nurse tells about a deeply Christocentric man dying of lung cancer who was fighting death. He asked for water, moaned in despair, and voiced love for the family that had deserted him. The nurse realized she had been watching the stages of Jesus's passion: "I thirst," "Why hast thou forsaken me?" and "Father, forgive them, they know not what they do." She was inspired to ask, "Can you match Jesus's final words? Have you said, 'Into Thy hands I commend my spirit'?" With that he smiled, took her hand, surrendered to Spirit, and died.

On the other hand, a dying person's words can be a living testament. Early Friends would gather the entire household, children and visitors alike, around the bedside to share in what they called "a time of indisputable ministry." The dying person, who was "neither fully a part of this world nor yet joined to the next, spoke to those around with an authority possessed by no ordinary person." The Friends took notes to record these teachings and in 1701, they published nine volumes in a collection called *Piety Promoted*. This spiritual practice was honored widely. Just as faith guided life, it supported living unto death.

For example, Mary Dyer, right before she was hung on Boston Common, declared, "No ear can hear, no tongue can speak, no heart can understand the... refreshings of the spirit of the Lord which now I enjoy." John Woolman said as death approached, "I feel Thy power now, and I beg that in the approaching trying moment, Thou wilt keep my heart steadfast unto Thee." Edward Burrough murmured at the end, "Now my soul and spirit is centered in its own being, with God, and this form of person must return from whence it was taken." Famously, George Fox kept preaching to the end. Two days before he died, he proclaimed, "All is well, and the Seed of God Reigns over all, and over Death itself; and that tho' I am weak in Body, yet the Power of the Lord is over all, and over all disorderly Spirit."

Today also, people tend to gather around a deathbed. If that is taken to be a sacred space, ministry can flow both ways. Those present can offer spiritual support. And in your going, you can touch their lives. You might well open them to mystery and leave them unafraid to die.

Finding the Voices

Edward Burrough (1662), as quoted in Lucy Screechfield McIver, *A Song of Death, Our Spiritual Birth: A Quaker Way of Dying*, Pendle Hill Pamphlet 340 (Wallingford, PA: Pendle Hill Publications, 1998).

Katy Butler, *The Art of Dying Well: A Practical Guide to a Good End of Life* (New York: Scribner, 2019).

Diana Campbell of Alice Springs Meeting, Australia Yearly Meeting, email communication, October 24, 2022.

Mary Dyer (1660), as quoted in Horatio Rogers, *Mary Dyer of Rhode Island, the Quaker Martyr That Was Hanged on Boston Common, June 1, 1660* (Providence, RI: Preston and Rounds, 1896).

Quentin Fowler, Barbara Henderson, Paul Henderson, Judy Kessler, and Jill Page, eds., *Assisted Dying: A Quaker Exploration* (Leeds, United Kingdom: Leeds Area Meeting, 2016).

George Fox (1690), as quoted in Jane Mace, *Passion and Partings: The Dying Sayings of Early Quakers* (Petergate, York, UK: Quacks Books, 2020).

Carl Magruder, "On Quaker Deathways: Practices Around Death and Dying," July 14, 2022, in *QuakerSpeak*, produced by Rebecca Hamilton-Levi and Friends Publishing Corporation, https://quakerspeak.com/video/deathways.

Marcelle Martin, "Touched by Death and Dying," *Friends Journal* (October 2022), https://www.friendsjournal.org/touched-by-death-and-dying.

Lucy Screechfield McIver, *A Song of Death, Our Spiritual Birth: A Quaker Way of Dying*, Pendle Hill Pamphlet 340 (Wallingford, PA: Pendle Hill Publications, 1998).

The New English Bible with the Apocrypha (New York: Oxford University Press and Cambridge University Press, 1970), Isaiah 43:2.

Piety Promoted in a Collection of the Dying Sayings of Many of the People Call'd Quakers, with a Brief Account of Some of Their Labours in the Gospel, and Sufferings for the Same (1701), as quoted in Jane Mace, *Passion and Partings: The Dying Sayings of Early Quakers* (Petergate, York, UK: Quacks Books, 2020).

John O'Donohue, *Walking in Wonder: Eternal Wisdom for a Modern World* (New York: Penguin Random House, 2018).

William Penn, *Some Fruits of Solitude* (1682), as quoted in New England Yearly Meeting of Friends, "Dying, Death, and Bereavement," *Interim Faith and Practice* (Worchester, MA: New England Yearly Meeting, 2014), Chapter 6. https://neym. org/faith-and-practice/dying-death-and-bereavement.

Cole Arthur Riley, *Black Liturgies: Prayers, Poems, and Meditations for Staying Human* (New York, Convergent, 2024).

Bradford Smith, *Dear Gift of Life: A Man's Encounter with Death,* Pendle Hill Pamphlet 142 (Wallingford, PA: Pendle Hill Publications, 1965).

Susan Johns Smith, email communication, June 27, 2020.

Frances Taber, personal communication, April 6, 2023.

Elizabeth Gray Vining (1978), as quoted in Philadelphia Yearly Meeting of the Religious Society of Friends, *Faith and Practice* (Philadelphia: Philadelphia Yearly Meeting, 2017), "Extracts on Faith Reflected in Practice and Daily Life," #186.

Benjamin J. Wood, "Autonomy and dignity: A Quaker theological response to assisted dying," in Quentin Fowler, Barbara Henderson, Paul Henderson, Judy Kessler, and Jill Page, eds., *Assisted Dying: A Quaker Exploration* (Leeds, United Kingdom: Leeds Area Meeting, 2016).

John Woolman, *The Journal and Major Essays of John Woolman*, ed. Phillips P. Moulton (New York: Oxford University Press, 1971).

John Yungblut, *On Hallowing One's Diminishments*, Pendle Hill Pamphlet 292 (Wallingford, PA: Pendle Hill Publications, 1990).

Chapter 3

Gifting the Future

Our assets and debts, our property, our things, may be important to society and even to our nearest and dearest, but our living examples far outlast those things. The Quaker practice of living in harmony with one's values… is among our greatest gifts.

—John Surr, 2023

From my mother I inherited an artist's attention to detail and beauty and a poet's love of language. From my father I inherited tenderness and perseverance. I prize these parts of their legacy above all.

—Anonymous, 2023

In her will, my mother gave me a special sum to keep under my own name. "Even in the best marriage," she wrote, "a woman should always have something all her own." That means a lot to me—not just because I can travel, but because it lets me feel at once independent and warmly upheld.

—Anonymous, 2022

Advices written out of the 1756 London Yearly Meeting suggested that all earthly matters should be kept in order so that in their time of dying Friends would not be distracted from the holy work of seeking God.

—Lucy Screechfield McIver, 1998

Mother tucked a note in her desk for my brother and me to find after she was gone. It simply said: "Remember me in life. Not in death."
—Jim Riley, 2023

Everyone must leave something behind when he dies, my grandfather said. A child or a book or a painting or a house or a wall built or a pair of shoes made. Or a garden planted. Something your hand touched some way so your soul has somewhere to go when you die, and when people look at that tree or that flower you planted, you're there.
—Ray Bradbury, 1953

Make your life be your art and you will never be forgotten.
—Charlotte Eriksson, 2015

No one goes on, but what we leave behind keeps us alive for someone else.
—Adam Silver, 2018

How is your life a gift to the future? "Legacy" in the legal sense means the material things you leave behind when you die. We can look at legacy in a far broader sense, though, encompassing both the material and the spiritual.

No matter how rich or poor you are, you have a legacy, and you have already given most of it: your genes, if you have children; your energy and insight; your good works; the transformative power of your friendship, example, and outreach. Your legacy includes stories that will be told about you down the years; the ways you changed your family, other groups, and the wider community; plus the invisible gifts your being alive gave to people you don't even know you touched. The world is wholly different because you have been in it.

The way your life has spoken is the biggest gift of all. When you think about your impact on the future, your life story and the patterns of your living are far more important gifts than the material things you leave.

This chapter lays out the practicalities of the remainder of your legacy: your material gifts to the future. First we discuss documents that apply while you are alive. Then we explore making gifts after you die, through estate planning and through gifting your organs and body.

POWER OF ATTORNEY

Planning begins with accepting your limitations. A time might arise when you need help to manage your affairs. Perhaps you will be recovering from a stroke. Perhaps you will become unable to balance your bank account. Who will stand in for you?

A *power of attorney* (POA) is a document in which you appoint an *agent* to make financial decisions during your lifetime if you are unavailable or unable to make them yourself. This is not an estate planning document, though it is a first step on the way to estate planning. This document can be useful all through your life.

The document itself gives your agent authority to manage your financial affairs on your behalf when you can't. The power of attorney can meet your needs in many ways. Your agent could change the beneficiary on your life insurance, sell a car, or tap into your retirement account to pay medical bills. (A medical power of attorney, described in Chapter 2, is quite different.)

A *general durable power of attorney* provides your agent with broad powers. It is general because it covers any financial situation and durable because it continues to be valid as long as you live. However, it is wise to ask your financial institutions whether they accept this kind of POA. Some states allow banks and other financial institutions to require their own proprietary documents.

A *limited power of attorney* is created for a specific purpose, such as giving your agent the power to sell a car or rent a house for you.

A *springing power of attorney* becomes valid at a specified time, such as when you authorize it, or when two physicians certify that you are unable to manage your financial affairs yourself.

Despite the name, your agent does not have to be an attorney. Sometimes, though, an agent is called an *attorney-in-fact*. Often a family member, a good agent is practical, entirely reliable, and aware of your values. Ask whether the person you want to choose is willing to serve in this way. Find a tactful way to let the rest of the family know who will fill this role.

It is important to understand that your agent will have as much power to manage your assets as you do. If you must choose between an agent who has a head for business and one who has an unquestionable moral character, absolutely choose the trustworthy person.

It is an act of love to accept so much power—and an act of faith to hand it over. If this worries you, consider what will happen if there is no power of attorney in place. If you become incapable of managing your own affairs, your family might have to petition the court to name somebody as your guardian. Defining incapacity is tricky; the court process takes several weeks, and it is expensive. The court might choose someone you would not want. Far better to choose the help you prefer to rely on. Consider it a fulfillment of the testimony of stewardship and a wise gift to your future self.

Help yourself now and your agent later by recording where your money is kept and what bills get paid and when. List passwords, account numbers, automatic payments, PINs, and important contacts, including your family, business partner, insurance agent, accountant, and lawyer. Some resources for organizing this practical information are in "Readings and Support" in the Treasury of Resources. Keep the list up to date; passwords change frequently. Your executor or trustee will wind up needing the same information.

Power of attorney documents normally list an alternate in case your first choice of agent is unable or unwilling to serve when the need arises. Each state has specific rules about whether these documents must be notarized, whether they must be signed before witnesses who are not the agent or alternate agent, and how many witnesses are required.

Once you have created a power of attorney, remember to review the document periodically. Your choice might shift with circumstances. Is your agent still alive and willing? Still your best option? Remake it after ten years; an older document might not be recognized any more.

In all cases, the powers of your agent end with your death. Then your executor or trustee takes over.

ESTATE PLANNING

Estate planning is a practical extension of your spiritual legacy. It is the process of deciding what you want done with your assets—your physical and financial possessions—after you die. How will they be preserved, managed, and distributed? Making these decisions and documenting them in a way that is legally binding are what is meant by estate planning.

Why Should You Plan?

Estate planning is not just for the wealthy. Far more than an exercise in finance and law, planning how to pass on your assets asks you to examine who and what you value in your life. Who are the people you love, and what are the places and causes you love? How do you want to affect them beyond the limit of your own lifetime?

Planning your estate gives you agency far into the future. It is a tangible affirmation of what has abiding value for you. It is an act of tenderness for and trust in those to whom you decide to give. It smooths the way for those you leave behind and eases the tax burden, work, confusion, or contention that can arise with a death. It is also an act of faith: contemplating the time when you must let go of everything, you become less encumbered by things and more willing to entrust yourself wholly to Spirit.

Do not put off these opportunities. Rather than shying away from planning, take time to find the leadings of your spirit. Then follow them.

Identifying Your Estate

Your estate consists of everything you control upon your death. Whatever you have been able to save and accumulate is your estate. Examples are your home, land, car, personal property such as art or books, and financial accounts, savings, investments, life insurance, retirement funds, and annuities.

What is yours to give? It is important to identify each asset and to look at how each asset is titled. For example, whose name is on the deed to your home? On the title to your car? How about your bank accounts, IRAs, investment accounts, and insurance policies? Who may open your bank vault? Is each thing yours individually, do you share ownership, or do you hold it in trust? If the answers surprise you, you can correct the situation now.

For example, property owned jointly often falls to the surviving owner. A house held jointly with a spouse will belong to the surviving spouse, regardless of any distribution specified in an estate plan. That might not be what you want for this particular asset. Clarifying ownership and control of assets is an important starting point for estate planning.

Be aware that your debts might create a nest of complexity after your death. Perhaps you want to simplify matters by taking care of them while alive.

It is wise to make a descriptive listing of your estate and keep it up to date. Store this list in a safe place, such as a fireproof box at home or a safe deposit box at a bank. Let your agent have a copy. Your executor also will need it. You will find that the list helps you meet the future, too.

This overview can change the spirit in which you go forward. Is retirement possible? Are things you dream of doing more affordable than you supposed? Do you need to be more frugal? Are you moved to be more giving? Is every asset on your list still meaningful to you?

Of course, most of your personal property won't make it onto a formal list of assets. Perhaps, though, the act of listing will inspire you to look at what else you have amassed. Has some of it—perhaps boxed in the bottom of your closet—outlived its usefulness? Would some of it be a delight to regift? What have you neglected that is worth reclaiming? Taking stock can help you refocus on possessions with true meaning. You might write notes to accompany your father's watch and your grandmother's shawl, so their meanings will be conveyed to the future.

Writing a Will

If you were tempted to skip over this part, or this whole "legal" chapter, take a deep breath. All of this chapter is a necessary, specific piece of a love story. By writing a will, you affirm that your love reaches beyond your years.

Signing your will formalizes a loving connection. You are the momentary guardian of valuable things you willingly pass to others you care about, who will pass them to others in turn. You become part of what a Friend calls "the long hand-holding chain," practicing the testimonies of stewardship and community.

A *will* is a formal legal document that distributes your estate upon your death—unless you have allocated your assets by joint ownership, beneficiary designation, or trust, alternatives which we explore shortly. A will is a matter of public record, and everything it stipulates will occur under the supervision of a court. A will must be in writing, signed by the "testator," and witnessed in writing by two persons not otherwise named in the will. You can rescind a will by making a new one or amend a will by a *codicil*—an addition, also so signed and witnessed.

The will first names an *executor* who will take care of your estate. The executor takes over where a power of attorney ends. You want an executor who is calm, diplomatic, and impartial, above any family rivalries. Choose someone who is careful and sees projects all the way through. Consider whether the person you want is likely to survive you. Ask whether the person you want to choose is willing to serve.

The will identifies your *beneficiaries* and describes what each receives from your estate. Of course, your beneficiaries might include charitable, religious, educational, and other organizations, as well as individuals. Take special care to name children you mean to include who have not been formally adopted. Be sure to name a partner who might not otherwise have legal standing in your state. If you mean to include your step-grandchildren among your descendants, say so explicitly.

In your will, you may also name a guardian for your minor children or children with disabilities. If those children are teenagers when you die, the court will consider your wishes along with your children's preferences in naming a guardian.

You might also choose to prepare a *memorandum* designating who inherits items of special personal property, such as art, jewelry, or other heirlooms. If the estate is passing by will, the memorandum is binding and will go through probate along with everything else.

What happens if you die without a will? You lose the power to direct your legacy. All jurisdictions have an "intestacy" process. It names which relatives will inherit your estate. It prescribes what happens to the estate if there are no surviving relatives. A will is your gift to the future.

Keep the witnessed original of your will in a safe place. Give copies to your agent, executor, and lawyer. Let them know where to find the original. If it is in a safe at home, give them the combination. Don't store your witnessed original will in a bank. The bank will secure a safe deposit box upon your death until a court authorizes the executor to open it, but the court cannot designate an executor without a copy of the will.

Consider updating your will when there is a birth, adoption, divorce, or death, or some other major change in your life circumstances. Shred earlier versions of the will and replace copies you have given to others.

Understanding Probate

Except for the smallest estates, every will goes through probate. *Probate* is the process by which a court records a will and supervises carrying out its instructions. Each state has its variations, but the process is similar everywhere.

To begin the probate process, the will must be brought in person to the court or agency of the county of your legal residence at time of death. A clerk puts the will on public record. The court recognizes the executor you named to oversee your estate, providing a document to authenticate this role.

This executor will now identify and appraise all the assets in your probate estate, pay all debts and applicable taxes on behalf of the estate, make distributions to beneficiaries, and deliver a report to the court when this work is complete. This is not a small favor to ask of someone! Be sure to talk this responsibility over with the person you choose. It is helpful if the executor lives in the same state as the court.

In Virginia and West Virginia, probate generally lasts between nine months and two years. Probate is often shorter in Maryland, Pennsylvania, and Washington, DC. However, a complex estate might be in probate for several years. There might be substantial fees and court costs. For these reasons, you could explore passing on some assets in different ways.

Transferring Assets in Other Ways

There are three ways to transfer assets without going through a will. It is worthwhile to discuss these options with professionals. Assure yourself that these gifts will be received in the future as you intend.

Perhaps in your heart the home you share with family belongs equally to all of you; the car you let your daughter drive is virtually hers; the basement where you give your best friend refuge is his for as long as he needs it. This is generosity, but this is not how inheritance law works.

Who has rights of survivorship for each of your assets? You might decide to make portions of your estate—such as your house, car, or savings account—*joint property*. Such property normally is not governed by a will but passes automatically to the surviving joint owner. This can be a tremendous help to the survivor, saving time, effort, and major stress. It also saves money in the probate process. This is an ideal way to pass property between spouses, but if you use it to transfer property to the next generation, there sometimes are unintended consequences.

A second simple form of transfer is *beneficiary designation*. All bank and brokerage accounts can have a beneficiary. In most states, real estate and vehicles can also transfer by beneficiary designation. This is an effective way to transfer property without the probate process.

Be sure to review your choice of beneficiaries every few years. If, for example, one of your beneficiaries dies before you do or becomes incapacitated, you will need to make a change.

Trusts are a third alternative. Trusts are legal instruments that give control over specific property (financial, real estate, or other) to a trustee for the benefit of the beneficiaries.

There are many different kinds of trusts. A revocable living trust is created and takes effect during your lifetime, but it serves the same functions as a will after your death. During your lifetime, you retain control; you can act as your own trustee. You can revoke or amend the trust at any time while you maintain competency and capacity. You can put real estate and financial assets into your revocable living trust.

If you become incapacitated, a successor trustee will take over. The trust document will give your successor instructions about providing for your care during your disability. The successor trustee manages assets inside your trust, whereas your agent under a power of attorney manages assets outside the trust. Often, this is one person, wearing two hats.

If you want the revocable living trust to substitute for a will, name the trust as beneficiary of *all* your assets. The instructions in your trust will control what your beneficiaries inherit. You could include a binding memorandum. A short "pour-over will" would add anything you forget to put into the trust. Your trustee will gather assets, distribute them, and pay final expenses without going through probate.

There are many other kinds of trusts, serving a wide range of needs. For example, you could set up a charitable remainder trust; this means making a sizable gift to a tax-exempt organization and receiving regular payments during the remaining years of your life. Other options are creative or intellectual property trusts, Medicaid asset protection trusts, business trusts, and a trust for a minor or a person with a disability. If these are the right fit for your situation, a good estate planning attorney will guide you in creating them. The peace of mind that you will feel when your affairs are in order is a wonderful gift to yourself and your family.

Finding Legal Help

Reading this chapter is a good beginning, but it is not a substitute for professional help. Now you have a head start on estate planning and compelling reasons to follow through with it. Each document will confirm your values, your spirit, and your love. Each document will be a gift to yourself and a gift to the future.

Once you have thought things through, find a qualified estate planning attorney or an elder law attorney to make sure everything is in order for the future you want. Choose an attorney in your own state or jurisdiction. There are differences in laws, terminology, and taxation from one jurisdiction to another, with substantial legal consequences.

For Friends who can't afford an attorney, many legal aid offices and senior centers offer clinics to create simple wills. Look for opportunities in your community to work with a pro bono attorney to create valid, functional documents. This is one time when relying on the internet is ill-advised. Do-it-yourself estate planning is a really bad idea.

The Treasury at the back of this book has a list of legal resources in the "Readings and Support" section. With the right help, estate planning will not be a formidable process, but a reassuring and empowering one. Way will open.

BEYOND THE WILL

Remember that inheritance entails both the law and the spirit. Here are a few heartfelt means of enhancing your legacy.

Letters of Instruction and Ethical Wills

You can supplement your legal estate planning documents by writing a *letter of instruction* to be opened just before or after your death. Such a letter is not a legal instrument, but a valuable personal communication.

Indicate on the envelope when you want it to be opened. A letter with instructions about final care, burial, or a memorial service should be opened *before* you die. It might say, "I want to die in my own bed," or "I want my grandson to play piano at my memorial." A letter of love can be opened whenever you choose.

A letter can be more specific than your will: "I want Susan to have Aunt Minnie's brooch, because there was a special bond between them." Or "Let my son have first choice of my music collection, because we shared that passion." It can tell how you intend your legacy: "I am praying that you will use this legacy to give each of my grandchildren the education I never had."

You might also write an *ethical will.* This is a message from the heart. It passes on to your loved ones some of your values. It has no legal standing, so it can be devised in any form that is expressive for you. It might be a letter, audio file, artwork, or video. Also called a *legacy letter*, an ethical will is a way to share the moral and spiritual foundations of your life, the guiding principles for the decisions you made, and the joys and satisfactions you had. It might offer a statement of inner leadings that resonated through your life, or it might sum up your hopes for your loved ones.

Tuck these special documents, or an explanation of where to find them, in with your other planning documents. Your family will be grateful for your voice when the time comes. These personal statements often become a treasured part of family history.

Gifts with Warm Hands

Once you have considered the legal instruments of inheritance, you might find that you are moved to give more while you are still alive. If you make gifts "with warm hands," you could watch your dear ones enjoy your generosity. You could give a young potter money toward building a kiln, or a child the assurance of a debt-free college education. You can give away up to the annual federal gift tax exclusion amount ($18,000 per recipient in 2024) each year without any tax consequences.

If you have enough assets for your own security, our Quaker testimony of simplicity might guide you to shed some of the excess wealth and material possessions you have accumulated over your lifetime. Seeing your gifts doing good in your family and community could bring you deep satisfaction.

GIFTING YOUR BODY

An extraordinary expression of the testimonies of stewardship and community is the gift of your physical body. One donor can save and heal as many as seventy-five lives.

Signal your intention to donate your body on your driver's license. Also write it in your advance directive; if you do not see a place, write it in at the end of the directive. Be sure to tell your doctor, your health care agent, and your family. As the time of death approaches, their cooperation will be vital.

Major organ donations—kidney, liver, heart, and lung—answer a tremendous need. There are well over 100,000 people on the national active transplant waiting list, and seventeen people die each day in the United States waiting for organ transplants.

You can make major organ donations only if you die in the hospital. When death is impending, the hospital is required by law to inform the regional Organ Procurement Organization (OPO) of a potential donor. There ensues an intense process of verification, working with the family for approval, and setting up a tightly coordinated plan for transplanting as many organs as possible.

Coordination between the hospital and the regional OPO is usually swift and smooth, taking one to three days, during which the hospital is instructed to keep the patient alive on life support. Extensive teams are needed, sometimes across many states, for delicate removals, timely transport, and ultimate transplantation.

If you die at home, you cannot donate any of these major organs. You must weigh your wish to die at home without medical interventions against your desire to be a donor. Be aware of this tradeoff.

There are no age limits for major organ transplant donors. Sadly, the most valued organs are those of healthy young adults who die in an accident, especially from head injuries. Both parents must consent for a minor's organs to be donated. But at any age, as long as you are terminal and do not have an infection or cancer, your heart, liver, and other organs could be accepted.

One major organ donation takes a different path. *Brain banks* welcome the brain of anyone over eighteen, regardless of where the person dies. It goes not for transplant but for research about neurological disorders, such as addiction, autism, epilepsy, schizophrenia, dementia, and Parkinson's disease. Such a donation is useful whether or not you suffer from one of these diseases. It is necessary to enroll in advance with the Brain Donor Project. This registry serves the National Institute of Health's NeuroBioBank, a national network of brain banks. They can recover the brain either at a medical center or at a funeral home.

If you want to make *tissue donations*, you can die at home or in a hospital. Some tissues remain viable for several hours, even without blood flow. Family or a doctor must notify the OPO. Skin, the largest organ, is sorely needed for burn patients, cleft palate repair, and mastectomy reconstruction. Tissue banks can store skin for up to five years. Corneas are universally useful, so long as the donor was not blind at death; there is no need to match donor to recipient. Ninety-seven percent of corneal transplants are successful in restoring vision. Donated veins and arteries can save a limb from amputation. Other transplantable tissues include the middle ear, heart valves, bones, cartilage, tendons, and ligaments.

Medical devices like pacemakers, defibrillators, artificial joints, and dental implants are often reusable. Many refurbished cardiac devices go to help low-income patients. Ask your cardiologist to assist you with such a donation. Preferably, donated pacemakers have at least 70 percent of the original battery life. The University of Michigan Medical School collaborates with World Medical Relief to supply used pacemakers and defibrillators through Project My Heart Your Heart. (See https://myheartyourheart.org.) An added benefit of this reuse is keeping toxic lithium batteries out of the environment.

Metals are recycled in manufacturing or reused in new prosthetics. Gold, silver, titanium, platinum, and cobalt can all be recovered. If you are inclined to participate in such reclamation, choose a crematory or funeral home that practices recycling; they will remove metal parts before proceeding with arrangements.

If you donate your *whole body* to science, you help to train medical students or support research. Either way you touch many lives in future generations. You must register in advance of death with a nearby medical school or with your state's anatomical board. Nearly everyone qualifies, with no age limit. Bodies will be disallowed only if there was recent surgery, infectious disease, autopsy, extreme obesity or emaciation, or removal of organs for transplant. A whole-body donor can die at home.

If you make a whole-body gift, your family typically receives cremains a few months to a year later. Georgetown University School of Medicine holds an annual memorial service around Thanksgiving to give thanks for all the cadavers its students have been able to study.

Many Friends feel good about donating their physical bodies to help another person live or to advance science. It means your love continues, literally embodied, in the lives of others whom you have never even met. This can also comfort your family. As one Friend puts it, "For me that would be a spiritual choice. There is no greater gift."

Finding the Voices

Ray Bradbury, *Fahrenheit 451* (New York: Ballantine Books, 1953).

Charlotte Eriksson, *Another Vagabond Lost to Love: Berlin Stories on Leaving & Arriving* (Scotts Valley, CA: CreateSpace Publishing, 2015).

Lucy Screechfield McIver, *A Song of Death, Our Spiritual Birth: A Quaker Way of Dying*, Pendle Hill Pamphlet 340 (Wallingford, PA: Pendle Hill Publications, 1998).

Jim Riley, personal communication, 2023.

Adam Silvera, *They Both Die at the End* (New York: Quill Tree Books, 2018).

John Surr, personal communication, 2023.

Chapter 4

Circles of Care:
The Primary Caregiver

To live in this world
you must be able
to do three things:
to love what is mortal;
to hold it
against your bones knowing
your own life depends on it;
and, when the time comes to let it go,
to let it go.

—Mary Oliver, 1983

Dying can be one of love's finest moments.
—Shulamith Clearbridge, 2023

Faith and hope are not about believing everything will be all right. They call us to our purpose: to love one another. They call us to constantly cultivate love in quiet ways through it all.… In turn, faith and hope promise us that no matter what happens, unexpected tangible support will arrive, joy and love will comfort us, and infallible guidance will lead us every step of the way.

—Judith Goedecke, 2019

Sixty-five years ago, I said "I do." And this difficult work, my care-giving, is how I *do* it now.

—Geraldine Cunningham, 2023

Simple routines done lovingly are liturgy—a ritual of two souls who are living out their "yes" made many years before. That divine life we call "the Light" is my daily trysting place.

—John Guiser, 2019

What we must do with God's help, is to accept sorrow as a friend, if possible; if not, as a companion with whom we will live for an indeterminate period; a companion of whom we shall always be aware but with whom we can work, from whom we can learn, and whose strength will become our strength.

—Elizabeth Gray Vining, 1952

They that love beyond the World cannot be separated by it. Death cannot kill what never dies.

—William Penn, 1682

CAREGIVING IS ARGUABLY THE MOST INTIMATE act of all. Serving as primary caregiver can be the most challenging and the most rewarding thing you ever do.

Accompanying a death is a little like midwifing a birth. Both involve labors—slow or fast, smooth or difficult. Both involve a great transformation happening to another's body and soul. It might be a person with whose body you are intimate—a child, a parent, or a lover. Even if this is a person you don't like, it is hard to watch suffering. Your job is to support, advocate, coach, validate, inter-vene—and allow.

Nothing bigger or more demanding has ever been asked of you. You are deeply aware, actively responsive, but not in charge.

Quakers open to what is, and let Spirit have its way. You are part of a holy process.

BECOMING THE PRIMARY CAREGIVER

If you are fortunate, caregiving is the natural culmination of years of love, in which you have always supported each other's transformations. You throw yourself into the part. You want to love your dear one all the way through to the last change, in every way possible. If you are fortunate, there will be enough time to find the way forward gently and together.

But sometimes you do not know the other deeply—it's the isolated man across the street, or a second cousin, or an acquaintance with nowhere else to turn. You search your spirit and find compassion. You discover a leading to serve. There will certainly be gifts for you, hidden within this service.

At still other times, the decision is made for you. You are the only child of an aging parent, or the child who lives closest or seems least busy, so you are expected to step up. Or perhaps no one else can be conscripted to care for a relative who is abusive. Even if you believe you are not suited to this job, you are tapped. Trust that even here you might discern the hand of God in time.

What if you want to say, "No, this work is not for me"? You might feel inadequate, or squeezed by other responsibilities, or burned out from other caregiving. You might be exhausted and need a break. Saying no does not have to mean that you are abandoning someone. Guilt need not be a part of asserting healthy boundaries.

From the Quaker perspective, this resistance is a "stop." It calls for a pause to examine what else is happening. When you listen to Spirit, it speaks through such stops, redirecting you to a previously unimagined way forward. Talk it through with a trusted friend, and if feasible, with the person who needs care. Name the level of engagement you are comfortable with, and find other ways to provide care. You can honor the relationship without being the full-time caregiver.

If you say yes, your first challenge is spiritual: finding the inner grace to affirm this calling, in spite of discomfort. This person's suffering is the last thing you want to witness. You don't mean to lose anyone on your watch. But this is a job that includes losing. Perhaps you find yourself shaking a fist at heaven. Can you carry on a passionate dialogue with the Divine while you do its will? Can you accept that you are going to lose this person, and it's going to happen right in front of you? Can you accept how this person's mortality makes you suddenly more mortal yourself?

You also need grace to accept your own part. As primary caregiver, your life is going to be turned upside down. For a time—a finite time that might be all too short or feel interminable—your waking hours, even your sleep cycle, will be less and less your own. Your strength, your instincts, your stamina, your humor, your patience, your skill at communicating: every bit of these will be tested and sometimes exhausted. What a job description!

How you answer the call makes all the difference. Perhaps you are so shaken by the idea of the coming loss that you can't imagine going forward. Can you decide to trust that grace will arise for both of you, whenever it is needed? Perhaps you feel deep self-doubt or long-held resentment, even rage. Can you lay your own history, or the history between the two of you, to rest? Perhaps you remember a terrible experience with death. Can you look steadfastly at its lessons now and decide to give this death a different shaping?

Above all, can you allow yourself to be good enough but not perfect? Can you commit to try your hardest, knowing you will make mistakes? You will certainly have a meltdown sometime along the way. Only agree to be Love's imperfect instrument.

For many Friends, discerning this calling and following through with it are helped immeasurably by turning themselves over to Spirit. One Friend says, "There is no way I could have done this without making time every day for meditation and prayer."

PRACTICING PRESENCE

Becoming a primary caregiver means taking on physical work, which can be demanding and relentless. At the same time, it calls for a labor of the spirit.

Companioning another in the face of death asks you to practice the *ministry of presence*. A term often used by hospice chaplains, this means listening deeply with compassion, with tenderness and without judgment, meeting the other in that which is eternal. Simply by being there—physically, emotionally, and spiritually—you offer calm and comfort. You validate the sacredness of the other.

Holding another in the Light without ceasing becomes your focus. You can do it while your heart is breaking. You have powerful feelings that deserve to be addressed, but the ministry of presence is not about you. You are present to offer understanding, not to be understood. Your prayers for yourself are about patience, compassion, and endurance.

You practice presence in the smallest act. Kirsten Backstrom says of a woman in hospice,

> I listened with my hands when I brushed her hair and tried to sense what felt good to her and what did not, when to continue and when to stop. I listened with my eyes when I looked about her room and at her face, and saw and felt the unique quality of her reticence and her dignity. As much as possible, I kept my own personality out of her way—and listened with my heart to the best of my ability.

You also practice presence in the largest sense, by accepting and supporting the spirituality of the person in your care. Perhaps you find it challenging to hold on to your own inner truth in the face of someone else's crisis. Or perhaps that person's steadfast faith deepens and anchors your own. Either way, you just listen and ask tender questions. You give the other person permission to struggle, room to grieve, and time to grow into Light.

A New Relationship

The person in your care is going through change, so your relationship must change too. What makes this person familiar and dear to you might persist or even be heightened—but typically, abilities, behaviors, and even temperament undergo a shift, whether subtle or dramatic. "How do I do this," a Friend asks, "when he is changing right in front of me?" On what ground can you now stand? Ideally, the ground is your will to hold fast to love.

As you shift gears into increasing levels of caregiving, the person in your care might help your spirit cope—or not. In the best possible world, this is a new dance of love. The two of you share the experience, taking turns leading the way. If this is a loving marriage, you hold each other more tightly than ever. Each moment that can still be shared is precious. You exchange the unfolding truths of your situations. Each of you helps the other grow in spirit.

But just when communication is most precious, it is often least available. People who are declining might seem to be idle, but they are actually hard at work. At their own speed—not yours—they are facing mortality, fears, and losses, taking stock of the past and future in a new light, and struggling for grace. Their patience is being tested by daily indignities, and their strength for the simplest familiar task is diminishing. They are, most likely, just plain tired. Maybe they are disappointed in themselves. Maybe they give themselves over to inner work, to the laboriousness of once-easy physical activity, and to sleep. If yours is a full-time job of care, theirs is a full-time job too—a complex, epic challenge.

Or maybe they are expending their strength in avoidance. Denial, pride, shame, or sheer preoccupation might make them push help away, or take help for granted. Your task is to meet them where they are, allowing ambiguity and space for transformation. Perhaps you nudge gently, but mostly you hold them in the Light.

Caught up in personal changes, the one you care for might stop seeing you clearly. Yet perhaps this is the very person you have depended on to help you make meaning. Your spiritual challenge, then, is to begin to make meaning on your own, to trust who you will become apart from this essential partner.

Or perhaps this is a person who never saw you well at all, and time is going to run out on that possibility. Perhaps this is a person who does not communicate well, or the two of you have no practice of talking things over. Perhaps the person's capacity to think is dimming, and the ability and will to speak are ebbing. Then you have to intuit and accept much that is unsaid. You are witness to things the other cannot face or articulate. You have to do the work on both sides. You have to be both partners in the dance.

Becoming a parent to your parents can be a sweet reversal. One dying Friend smiled at her daughter and said, "I am your little girl now." On the other hand, if your parents did not nurture you, caregiving can be extremely fraught. They gave you no role model for nurturance. You are still inventing it, while you freshly grieve the lack. Caring for a parent who was abusive awakens old wounds and requires digging deeply into your spirit. As one Friend said, "I could not tend him out of love, but I could do it out of compassion." It is not inevitable, but it is conceivable that this difficult time together will open a way to forgive.

No matter what your relationship was, no matter what new form it is about to take, a good starting point is to say something like this: "I am here for you. I will do my imperfect best. Here I am, as I am, in the world as it is."

If you love the person in your care, you are going through a process of advance grieving. In a different way, the other is going through this too. A person with exceptional honesty, self-awareness, courage, and gallantry will share the process with you. If not, you must reach for those qualities in yourself. You can model communicating when the other cannot model it for you. It is powerful just to say aloud, "I love you so much, and this is so hard for me."

In this relationship there will be a constant shift. You are becoming more dominant in basic physical care. You are easing into doing a hundred things the person in your care used to do. Slowly or swiftly, you become the recordkeeper, the pill-giver, the money manager, the housekeeper, the driver—the list is endless. This is a shift in power. Part of your task is to find out that you are capable enough for two. Part of your task is to uphold how much the other person still matters.

One graceful response to this dilemma is to ask the person in care to mentor you. This affirms the other's wisdom and capability as you take over.

Another solution is to give way, allowing the other as much agency as safely possible. This calls for creativity. Your husband can't drive, but he can navigate. Your mother can't travel to her grandson, but she can read children's books over the phone. Make it a world that still contains choices: Bath today? Leave the door open? Have you had enough? This is to affirm the person who is still there beneath all the changes. It is to assure them that they are not less because they do less. They are still potent and important.

You are having to hold on more firmly than ever before; at the same time, you are having to detach more entirely than ever before. You have the illusion of assuming control, turning yourself into a living prosthesis—but in fact, your control is inexorably slipping. Another of your spiritual tasks is to reconcile this paradox.

Beneath it all, your spirit is preparing to give a great gift. You give up your claim upon the other's life. You assure the other that everyone and everything the person holds dear will be all right. You do more than grant permission: you affirm the right of the other to go ahead and die. You bless the going.

ACCEPTING SUPPORT

This sounds like a tall order, and it is, but you will learn in the doing. You bear the greatest weight, and caregiving is in some ways a lonely job, but you do not need to do it alone. Indeed, if you are to stay the course, you must not try to go it alone. As one Friend's mother advised, "Now is the time to call in all your resources."

Who needs help? Every caregiver. Working people don't have the hours to give full-time care. Cash-strapped people cannot afford to pay for companions, aides, or a facility. People who are not strong can't handle certain physical tasks. People with children are being pulled in two directions. People who are emotionally strained need time off. Even the best-equipped person needs respite.

When caregiving is simply a natural stage in a committed love, you want to do it all. You might not trust others to care as well as you do. But even a fully available, able, determined caregiver needs and deserves help. At the very least, you need help so that your own spirit is replenished and you can stay the course. At the same time, the person in your care needs the refreshment of interacting with other people. Having help is essential to succeeding.

However reserved your nature, however much you believe in self-sufficiency, it is good to make your situation known and to open yourself to help. Taking help is not an imposition; it is a gift to the helper. It is a sign not of weakness but of strength.

You don't have to wait for the mythical moment when things are "really bad." The idea is to balance work with relief so you won't crash. Ask for what you need, not just for your own sake, but for the sake of the person you are caring for.

Asking for help enlarges your capacity and your spirit. If you keep resisting help, it is part of your spiritual work to discover what holds you back. What is this "stop" telling you? Have you been taught to be strong at any cost? Are you possessive of the person in your care, especially as time grows short? Are you afraid of abandoning that person or of being abandoned? Have you fallen into a habit of hypervigilance, or a secret belief that if you are a superhero—if only you keep doing absolutely everything—your person cannot die?

Such patterns are long-standing and deep-seated. You might uncover them in the course of conversation, meditation, therapy, or prayer. Letting go of them lightens the spirit. This process can take a long time. One Friend says, "The angels are there for me, but they always wait to be asked." Another Friend notes, "It helps me to pray every single time I approach her bedside." In the ongoing act of allowing help, you ground yourself again and again in your most important role: to be present in love.

There are many layers of potential support. Family could be the first place to turn. After family come your friends. For many people, friends *are* a family. A third layer of support is communal. Make your situation known in all your communities: where you worship, work, play, and volunteer, plus the networks of the person in your care. A group can organize care on a more sustainable basis and a wider scale than a single friend.

The last layer of potential support is professional. A personal counselor, social worker, or chaplain might strengthen you or the person in care. A geriatric caseworker might assess the level of need. At some point the time might arrive for help from a facility—adult day care, assisted living, a nursing home, an inpatient hospice. If you accept such help, you do not become less of a caregiver; you only release certain practical aspects of care at necessary times.

Asking for help is part of the testimony of community. To dwell in community implies mutuality—not only giving but receiving. The more explicitly you ask, the more likely you will be to receive just what you need.

Support from Family

Ideally, the first layer of support is family. If you have a family, and if it is close-knit, you might have a ready-made team whose members are good at communicating and willing to help you and the person in your care. They can trade shifts so no one gets exhausted; they bring different skills and insights. The family can shore each other up.

Not every caregiver has that advantage. Family members might live far away. They might be in denial. They are often on different pages, grieving in advance, or reacting to their own versions of history. They might not want to have anything to do with family. Sibling rivalries might come into play. Perhaps they fear being "cut out of the will"; perhaps they are jealous of your closeness. Blended families can add complications to this situation.

As caregiver, you can call a family meeting to lay out the situation. Tell them what you need. You can name the boundaries for what care you can and cannot give. You can ask each family member for a specific form of support. You can learn each other's limits and work tenderly around them.

It is also helpful to schedule regular family calls to keep everyone aware and pulling together. These calls are occasions to include the person in your care, at the center of the action if possible. Is everyone listening well to that person? Is it time to reconfigure care?

It becomes crucial for family to labor together when the person in decline resists care. Some people insist on independence at all costs. They are willing to risk the consequences of falls and isolation, or they intend to go on damaging themselves with smoking, heavy drinking, drug abuse, eating the wrong foods, or not taking prescribed medicines. Are they within their rights? Are they depressed? Are they risking the well-being of others? To untangle the ethical and practical issues, the family might want to seek the counsel of elders or professional help.

Even a loving family might not be all the help you need. Grown-up children can be far away, tied up in making a living, or tending children of their own. Perhaps with a parent's decline, the bedrock of the family is crumbling, so grown children are leaving childhood behind again, in a new way. Just when you need their support, you might have to support them. You must be a teacher, referee, and comforter.

But the opposite also can happen: adult children surprise you. You might discover that they too need to participate, to make things a little better, to bond in the time remaining. These opportunities are their birthright. You might be gratified to see how well the children have matured. The gifts you once gave them are returned and multiplied, and they have had plenty of practice dealing with you and with the person in care. These children are tangible forms in which the many qualities of the family will survive. They have grown-up gifts you can lean on with gratitude.

What can you ask of younger children? Even the very young know something is happening, and that something is happening to them. They need reassurance that it is not their fault, or anybody's fault, and they are not being abandoned on purpose. Tell them that there is nothing they can do to change the outcome, but they can do something, however small, to make the way easier. Welcome them into the circle of care. Show them how love copes. This is an image of dying they will carry for the rest of their lives.

Don't expect young children to take over the household, and don't ask them to be perfect miniature grown-ups. Let them be their own age and express love and loss. It might look negative: tantrums, nightmares, bed-wetting. It might be beautiful: a drawing, a dandelion, the loan of a beloved toy. By simply lying down with the person in care, holding and being held, a child gives an immense healing gift. You can ask the young for a hug, for a song, for the refreshment of laughter, for remembering how to play, for the assurance of a future. Tell them Papa's story in simple terms, and it will help unravel the complexity of caregiving for you. Be sure you thank them for helping.

Support from Friendship

Friends have multiple roles: to support the caregiver, to support the family, to support the person in decline. These anchoring roles are explored in Chapter 5.

Though you might feel alone as a caregiver, you have more friends than you imagine. You will be surprised at who actually comes through with help and what a relief it is. As one Friend put it, "I appreciated that I could talk to my friends about what was happening. I didn't have to carry that weight alone."

The person in care has friends too, both known and unexpected, waiting to be drawn into the circle of care. Those friends might long for time one-on-one; but shy of stepping forward, they might worry and grieve at a distance.

Both you and the person you care for can get isolated. There is less and less time and energy for the interactions that used to be energizing and purposeful. It can get hard to find time and energy even to shower. Slowly the world shrinks down to a couple of rooms. Maintaining connection is a prime role for your friends.

Old friends remember who you are, outside the all-consuming role of caregiving. They know your whole story, into which this will fit in the end. They can bear witness to complaining and despair, and hold your best in trust. They can hear the unspeakable or say it aloud. Without pushing for cheer or falsifying the situation, they can say truly, "I know who you are. I never admired you more than now." This is a priceless gift.

Support from the Meeting

You can turn to the meeting community for ongoing support in caregiving. You can put out a call for practical help. Just as important is to ask to be held in the Light, to let the spirit of the whole community support your own spirit. Spiritual help could take form in a clearness committee for a difficult decision, a long-standing support committee, or a meeting for healing. These roles are explored in Chapter 6.

For example, one Friend asked, "Please help me keep my heart and soul together as I am becoming a widow." Soon a small group of Friends and a close neighbor were gathering once a week to support her with prayerful consideration of whatever she wanted to share. They met virtually during the pandemic. They continued to meet through her husband's death and for the next eighteen months until she was ready to lay down the concern.

Support committees spend time in silent worship, active listening, reflection, and worshipful discussion. The intent is to hold the person in the Light during a challenging transition, letting the Spirit lead. This too is the ministry of presence. It allows the person to be heard, become open to the truth beneath the words, and be anchored in a beloved community. Such committees are a tangible example of the Quaker vision of Gospel Order: the community gathers to discern how to go forward in accord with divine love.

When you face tender times, the fellowship of Quakers is particularly nurturing, because Quakers know the way *does* open. We are accustomed to living with the unknown, allowing ambiguity, and trusting the process. Reflecting on the testimonies with seasoned Friends will reassure and comfort you, especially when making hard decisions, such as whether to call hospice, request a Do Not Resuscitate order, or place someone in a nursing facility.

You could also ask other Friends who are caregivers for an extraordinary gift—a mutual spiritual friendship. Caregiving changes each of you to the core, and this kind of friendship notices, nurtures, and validates that transformative work.

Within such friendships, members agree to open their souls to one another, sharing their deepest dreams, hopes, doubts, visions, and faith experiences. They do not flinch from speaking the truth.

They form deep queries and affirm answers. They intuit and invite goodness in one another. As Margery Larrabee tells us, such friendship is a form of prayer.

GATHERING RESOURCES

When you are called to caregiving, you are entering a new world. Please think ahead to gather all possible resources—practical and personal. Do this in advance instead of waiting until you are desperate.

You are now the coordinator, the advocate, and the watchdog. To fulfill these roles, it is wise to create a central place for information, such as a loose-leaf or digital file. You will add to it frequently. List medications, note important changes and events such as falls, and write down specially monitored health details such as blood pressure. Such documentation is crucial; if you don't write it down, you won't remember it. You are in a position to gather more vital details than anyone else on earth. Good medical care depends on information like this.

You can follow your checklist of medications every day, and so can anyone who comes to help you. Nurses will welcome the information, emergency room doctors will be grateful for it, and pharmacists will use it to avoid medication errors. Even if the person enters a facility, you can use the list to make sure nothing gets overlooked.

In the same location, include simple directions for all special procedures you are doing, like caring for wounds, handling oxygen, feeding through a tube, or giving insulin. If necessary, your notes will let another person step into caregiving smoothly.

Also gather emergency numbers, questions, appointments, and paperwork there, in a single place. Include with your documentation your person's advance directive (see Chapter 2). Know who their health care agent is, how to reach the agent, what the medical orders are, and what your person wants. Keep hard copies easily available for EMS. This will let you carry out your role with confidence.

Educate yourself right away about the conditions to expect down the road. Websites of organizations like the American Cancer Society and the Alzheimer's Association outline the progression of a specific illness. Look far ahead, even while you make the most of the present. Learn, too, from caregivers who have done this before you. Remember, though, that no matter what you read or hear, your experience will be unique. No one else has your spirit, your history, or your relationship.

In light of what you learn, assess your personal strengths. You yourself are the greatest resource. You need all your qualities, rightly applied: your stubbornness and ability to give way, your fierceness and softness. What is natural to you, how will you have to grow, and how will it be wise to lean on others? Are you organized enough to manage multiple medications and doctors' appointments? Are you strong enough to help a person transfer from bed to chair, or from wheelchair to car? Are you brave enough to drive to dialysis in a snowstorm? What help do you see yourself needing?

What physical care will this relationship bear? Dignity and privacy are important. Will your relationship allow you to help with toileting? Do you want the intimate opportunity to handle bathing and toileting yourself, or is it better for paid caregivers to step in? If possible, engage the person who needs care in these decisions, as well as family. Bear in mind that, with dementia, it is wise to decide to engage help on the early side so that it will become familiar.

Needs can change suddenly, so start now to take stock of services. Does your cancer center have a navigator, social worker, or support group? Is there a source of free medical equipment? A group that offers rides to medical appointments? A program providing food, such as Meals on Wheels? A counselor who makes house calls to shut-ins? What volunteer organizations and agencies around you provide home assistance or respite care? Is there a source of caregiver training? Gather a list of potential resources. When you are not sure what to do, this list will give you a solid start.

Another piece of proactive thinking is to seek advice about places that do inpatient rehabilitation or skilled nursing. In the future, your person might well be hospitalized. When the time comes to leave the hospital, what places would you trust? Listing them now will make things far easier.

Take a steady look too at your financial resources. Is any paid care covered by insurance? If your person is on Medicare, is there supplemental insurance? Is there long-term care insurance? With the cost of in-home care so high, some caregivers sign a contract, document their hours, and let long-term care insurance repay their services.

Does your person have enough money to consider private care? Agencies can supply both home health aides and skilled nurses, but Medicare has limited home coverage, and private in-home care is costly. If care is affordable, is it time to get it? Will paid care improve the quality of life for you and for the person in care?

While you are considering money, be sure that a durable power of attorney is in place (see Chapter 3). This means that no matter what the person's condition, access to funds can continue.

It is crucial to gather information about how the person hopes to be laid to rest: cremation, conventional burial, or green burial. Have you talked it over? See "Considerations for Laying the Body Down" in the Treasury of Resources for information on each of these options. Is a choice recorded in the person's living will (see Chapter 2)? Many meetings use the form "Wishes for the End of My Life," also in the Treasury of Resources. Would the person be willing to fill that out? Any kind of burial costs money; does the estate have enough? Have arrangements been made yet? In the overwhelming time after a death, knowing what to do and having plans in order will be a great relief and a gift.

"Plan for the worst; hope for the best" is a common mantra of emergency management professionals. Some people see gathering resources as "jumping the gun"—focusing on problems that don't exist. But in accord with the testimony of integrity, it helps you face reality head on. It is also what the testimony of stewardship is all about. Looking ahead keeps you calm and ready, competent and responsive.

MOVING PAST HOME CARE

The person you care for might express a hope to remain at home to the end, surrounded by familiar things and people. This might be a cherished picture in your mind, too. You might want to hold on to the way things are, forever. Dying at home could be the norm in your culture, and sometimes it does happen, beautifully.

You might keep going at home with plenty of dedicated helpers, or with certified nursing assistants or skilled nurses if you can afford enough of them. Another means of staying at home, if your person qualifies and consents, is to bring in hospice (see Chapter 2). Hospice supports not only the patient but the caregiver and the family. For example, there might be support groups, social workers, and volunteers who allow a few hours of respite.

But what if you see the time approaching when you can't manage care at home? Nursing facilities usually have a long wait list, so advance planning pays off. Look for accreditation and for ratings from the Centers for Medicare & Medicaid Services (CMS). CMS tracks multiple quality measures of care, such as the ratio of skilled staff to patients or the number of falls and medical errors.

If at all possible, go to see potential placements yourself. Look and smell; is it clean? Ask about turnover of staff and patients, family satisfaction scores, and what therapies are offered. Seek evidence that patients are protected and treated with dignity, kindness, and attention. Find someplace experienced with your person's medical condition, welcoming to visitors, and close enough that you can visit easily. If possible, let the person in your care come with you or have a say in the choice.

Sometimes the decision to leave home is obvious, though you feel a pang at letting go. Dementia can make a person wander or become violent. Your person might have become incontinent or too heavy to turn. You yourself might have worn out or become ill. If you are wondering whether the time has come, the answer is yes.

At this moment, you have to reach deep for grace. You are providing safety and comfort in a new form; you are not failing or abandoning your charge. You are still the primary caregiver, though other hands are instruments of care.

You are freed from physical labor, but you continue caregiving. You are going to watch closely over the care the facility provides. You follow every development, always advocating for your person's wishes and humanity. You are free now to devote most of your energy to companionship. You bring to the bedside as much of home and love as possible. Maybe you bring friends or the dog, photographs and stories, roses and homemade pie. You bring your guitar and sparkling grape juice on New Year's Eve. You bring honesty and courage.

You get more rest, but your heart is breaking, a little or a lot. It is natural to feel relieved, or bereft—or both at once. The house is yours now, but it might feel unfamiliar. The apparatus of care, of closely paired lives, still surrounds you; but sounds, scents, interactions, and intense focus are gone. Now is an important time for family and friends to move closer, into the gap.

Know that even if your loved one does stay at home, a withdrawal from home will come anyway. Your person is moving from intimacy to separation. Leaving for another facility is only one outward sign of necessary departure. Let it be practice in the greater labor of letting go.

WITNESSING DEATH

When the person you care for is ready to die, do what you can to make it a holy time. Before you enter the room, center yourself. Take a deep calming breath, tuck the person into your heart, and walk in the Light. Visualize Light holding the person and holding yourself, all the way through. Chapter 2 describes what you might expect to see in the dying process.

If you find it distressing to witness the labor of dying, breathe slowly and refocus. The dying person, drifting away, might not be aware of the sights and sounds that trouble you. Though you can't always find it readily, inside the mechanics of dying there is a sacred core.

Allow your tears and your feelings. They are a natural expression of your love. Prayer or soft music might be comforting. It is common to touch the person tenderly. If you are so moved, you can even climb into bed and hold the person. Notice and follow the person's subtle responses to touch, music, and positioning.

Speak quietly. Tell the person what is happening—"I am going to moisten your lips," "I am going to keep holding your hand." Name the persons who are present—"Abuelo, it's Carlos," "Your sister is here." Be sensitive when speaking with others in the room; assume that the dying person can still hear.

Speak as your heart bids. Many dying persons and loved ones find it helpful to say goodbye. Say what you need to, in your own way. Trust that the person can hear you and feel your loving presence. If you believe that you will always be together in spirit, affirm it. Consider sharing these essentials, if you have not said them already: *I love you, I thank you, I forgive you, I ask you to forgive me. We will be all right. You have my blessing and my permission to go.*

Let each person who wishes it take a turn saying goodbye in private. If someone is at a loss how to act, gently show them how.

Be natural in the presence of a dying person. If the family loves to share stories and laughter and song, let them do that now. It is a comfort to the dying to feel that the family fabric will not tear, that life and love will go on.

Some people rally briefly before they die. There can be a fleeting return to ordinary consciousness and physical presence. This is not a miraculous recovery. If it enables a last clear exchange, that is a form of grace.

Dying persons sometimes wait until they have seen or spoken to someone in particular. Sometimes they choose to die surrounded by loving faces, but often they seem to hold on until they are alone. Don't beat yourself up if you miss the moment when they slip away.

The actual moment of death is often so simple and quiet that you might not even recognize it. If you busy yourself watching for the last breath, you could overlook how smooth and easy and grace-filled a transition can be.

People keeping vigil sometimes report a sudden lightness in the room, even elation. One Friend said that watching a peaceful death was like watching a shooting star.

Even after the death, continue to hold the space for love. You might feel an emptiness, or a continued sacred presence, or both.

Unless you want it to, a relationship does not end at death. Whether or not you were present in person, you can say hello or goodbye in your heart as often and in as many ways as you need. You can go right on speaking to the person all your life. You might be granted an extraordinary experience of the person's presence. You will have years to hold wonderful or hurtful memories in the Light, and to reach an understanding of the person's story.

A peaceful death is not granted to everyone. What about deaths that are exceedingly painful or violent? Begin by acknowledging the trauma. In time, it is possible to hold such a death in the Light. You make inside yourself a haven, both for yourself and for the person who has died. In a sense, you become a caregiver *after* death. There are even Friends who walk battlefields and locations of mass casualty to release souls whom they perceive as lingering to the Light.

DEATHCARE

Time halts for a moment at death, and the Light is close. In that timeless moment it can be deeply natural to sit in silent worship. Even when a death is expected and you thought you were ready, it still can be a shock that it really has happened. Sitting still is your body's way of absorbing the change.

Later on, you will be swept up in doing. Slow down now, and just be present. You'll never get this time back again.

When you are ready, move gently. You might embrace the person, straighten the covers, and close the eyes. You might wash the body tenderly and dress it in beautiful, comfortable clothes. Whether or not you believe the body is the person, setting it to rights feels like ministry.

You can do this alone, as an act of deep intimacy. You can do it as a shared ritual, including family young and old in a last physical interaction. If it is hard to be alone, ask someone to join you in deathcare, and even ask them to stay with you for several nights afterward.

With a home death, there is no urgency; you can take a few hours if you wish to sit with the body. Many traditions hold that the soul slowly withdraws from the body rather than leaving abruptly when the heart stops. You might sense such a withdrawal over hours or days. If so, you might decide not to move the body immediately after death. Hospitals sometimes allow time before the body is removed from the room, giving family members time to arrive for their good-byes. Just ask your nurse for such grace time.

One call is necessary. Within a couple of hours, call your doctor or hospice to certify death. The doctor will take care of tissue donations if that is the plan.

After a death, some Friends fall back on traditions from their cultures of origin. Maybe they cover the mirror, open a window for the soul to fly free, or start to plan a wake. You might find yourself led to create rituals of your own. One Friend placed flowers over his wife's heart, inside the body bag. Another played the Brahms *Requiem*.

Ritual can supply a familiar pattern and tell you what to do. It can cushion you and help carry you forward. It can begin to give your grief tangible shape.

GRIEVING

There is no one right way to grieve. It can last for months or for years. What follows is distilled from the hard-won experience of many Friends, but perhaps you would write it differently.

Grieving can be hard work. Be gentle with yourself. Rest well. Sleep is not just an escape; some of the work of grieving happens in sleep. Time after time sleep restores the body and pieces together the soul. Even if you feel indifferent to food, eat well, as if you are feeding your own child.

Grieving is solo work, but don't give in to loneliness. Talk to others with a similar story and an outlook that uplifts you. If you have a support committee, lean on it; if not, ask for help to create one. Make sure you get out and that you get some physical exercise. Accept at least some of the invitations that come your way, even when you don't feel like going, and invite friends when they don't think to invite you. If the social scene seems to revolve around couples, call someone to go with you to events. Outreach takes effort, especially when a strong connection is newly severed, but it is important to stay in the world.

Grief is selfish—it is supposed to be. Your grief belongs to you, and it is not to be compared with anybody else's. You do not have to "snap out of it" or ever apologize for grieving, but you do need to figure out a way to surround grieving with living.

Take a leave of absence from work if you need to and can afford it, but not from the work of love. Don't block out people who depend on you, or people who are grieving in their own ways. Sooner or later, caring for them will reconfirm your attachment to life in community.

If there was a progressive illness, you had a head start in grieving. Death catches you already in the midst of grief. You have grieved gradually for the old ways of being and of being together. Good days were sweeter than ever but came with a pang because they were growing rare. By contrast, if death was unexpected, grief slams you without warning.

Grief might be mixed with anger—"He promised me fifty years; how could he leave me?" It might be mixed with fear—"How will I manage all this alone?" And it might be mixed with unsettling surprises, as skeletons emerge from the closet.

Grief often is mixed with guilt. You might feel guilty that you did not manage everything perfectly on the person's behalf, or that you did not die in the person's place. Also, you might feel guilty that death was a relief. Although you longed for your person to live forever, you wanted the suffering to end.

Maybe the person you knew disappeared almost completely while alive. Perhaps as dementia progressed, you wound up caring for a vague, lost child or for a violent, angry person—the shell of the person you loved. Perhaps, as pain increased, medications put the person into a deepening fog. At some point, you just wanted your person to have peace.

Often, then, caregivers are grateful that it is over, whereas for more distant friends and family, the loss is fresher. Maybe relief seems inappropriate to them. Be kind to them and also hold true to yourself, with integrity. Every response is natural.

Practice in this case does not make perfect. Grief in advance cannot be complete—so do not be in a hurry to make major decisions, such as whether to sell the house and move someplace new. When you are levelheaded, at peace, and ready for a fresh start, you will know it.

Meanwhile, it might be up to you to see to the belongings of the person who died. Unless there are pressures (the lease is up next week), go at a gentle pace. Think of the person's things not as a burden or as junk, but as the quirky expression of a unique soul. Take time greeting the past, savoring the legacy you hand out, whether in large ways or tiny tokens, and stop whenever this work is overwhelming.

Listen to your heart: if something gives you comfort and connection, don't rush to part with it. This is not foolish. You can sleep with his soft sweater, drink from her favorite mug. Children might want some clothing item that still smells like Mommy or Daddy, or you might want to keep the stuffed animal your child used to carry everywhere.

Make time and room for grief. If you repress it, it will not go away. You do not have to perk up for anyone. You are not on anybody else's timetable. You do not get over grief or past it or even through it. It is part of your soul's fabric. You learn to befriend it.

In the first months (or however long it takes), it is common to replay the time together. One significant early task might be to forgive yourself. You will see in time that no one is a perfect caregiver. You rose to a physical, emotional, and spiritual challenge the best you could. Nothing really prepared you for the worst or for the rewards. Take the experience as a gift to the person you are becoming.

Later on, the task often shifts. How shall I honor the past but open myself to the future? Who am I, who will I be, apart from this relationship? What has this person done for me that I now take into myself? These questions are both quite practical and deeply spiritual. Let them season.

Some emotions are common, but grief defies sequence. Elisabeth Kübler-Ross famously named five stages of grief: denial, anger, bargaining, depression, and acceptance. Therese Rando defined six phases: react, recollect, reexperience, relinquish, readjust, and reinvest. In truth, there are many more steps than these, and the sequence is not linear. A bereaved person cycles between opposite feelings, or bumps about in a complex mix, or relives emotions they thought were "finished."

Emotion comes in waves, receding and returning. You can just pull over when a wave hits. Or you can set a limit to a particular wave, in order to function: "I will let myself keep crying until I reach the highway; I will cry the rest when I get home." You can set aside a time and place sacred to grief. But the waves will come for years. Using a different metaphor, one Friend says, "You get much better at walking on level ground, but still you stumble into holes you don't see coming."

Over time, for most people, the waves become less intense as they do the work of grieving and begin to create new lives. You also experience waves of ordinary happiness, which become stronger. Kahlil Gibran wrote, "The deeper that sorrow carves into your being, the more joy you can contain." Now and then you catch yourself laughing. Let it happen.

Years later, grief and remembered joy both could ambush you, out of the blue or at a regular season you come to anticipate. One Friend has official "Days of Grief and Remembrance," which span the anniversaries of losing her father, mother, and husband. She has written lifesaving advice and reassurance from herself to herself, which she staples to the calendar. Another Friend takes time off work for her husband's death day and their anniversary.

It can take a long time to disentangle some elements of grief. Every death you experience reawakens the memory of every other death, even those you think you put to rest long ago. In mourning for one, you mourn for all. It helps sometimes to recognize which grief is knocking you down. In this moment, are you really a seventy-year-old man mourning his best friend, or a six-year-old boy mourning his daddy, or both? What does the man need, and how can you comfort the child?

It is also natural to grieve for your lost role, who you were in the relationship which has "ended." Do not let society's word "widow" unwife you. If you were a wife, you are still a wife, for as long as your heart claims it.

The truth of your connection is undone only if you yourself choose to sever it. If you were a mother, you are forever a mother. If you were a daughter, you are still a daughter, not an orphan.

Whatever grief work you need, trust that doing it can lead not only to comfort but to transformation. If it was a loving relationship, you probably grieve being special, having an assured place in the center of someone's heart. One of your tasks, then, is to find that assurance in yourself. If you depended all your life on others for validation, this is groundbreaking spiritual work. If it was a hurtful relationship, you might well grieve the finality of rejection. One of your tasks might be to forgive. Another is to turn at last to sustenance in a new, wholesome form.

Almost all caregivers also are grieving for their own mortality. This death confirms it and brings your turn closer. If you have lost an elder, maybe no relative "protects" you now by going first. You are suddenly supposed to be the wise one—and the vulnerable one. If someone younger than you died, it brings home that no generation is safe. In the terrible case of losing your own child, the natural order, the succession in which you trusted, is upended; you grieve your place as the one who shields by going first. It turns out there is no protection.

Slowly, with growing integrity, a caregiver gives up the secret beliefs that underpin grieving: "I should have been the one." "If I had only loved him better." "No one will ever love me again." "It is wrong to feel happy." "I am afraid to be alone." "I hate God." Whatever your secrets are, you are not alone in suffering them, and you are called to yield them up. You do it by holding them in the Light, talking to the person who died, or keeping a journal. Or you do it in the presence of others: a support committee, spiritual friend, spiritual director, grief group, or counselor. The untruth in these beliefs washes away. A relief! What is left is compassion and love.

Since the work of grief is lasting, you might seek a recurrent way of remembrance across time, even down the generations. For example, in the Jewish faith, at every single service you can rise to recite the mourner's prayer. You also light a yahrzeit candle on every anniversary of a death. In Mexico, on the Day of the Dead, the living create personal, beautiful altars for those who died and picnic at the gravesite.

Inventing their own ritual, one Friend and her siblings meet for dinner and worship every year to celebrate their long-gone mother's birthday. To remember a woman who loved nature, another Friend takes a meditative walk along the river, scattering birdseed. One family who lost a daughter to brain cancer gathers each spring at the Race for Hope to raise money for research. They form a team carrying a banner with her name. Each event commingles loss with celebration.

You can also make a lasting symbol of remembrance. You might commit to wearing a cameo with your mother's picture, or a tattoo emblematic of your husband. In honor of your little sister, you could plant a white oak, which can live 400 years. The symbol prompts you to tell the person's story to each new acquaintance. Create whatever gives you comfort and continuity.

In the course of grieving, it is not uncommon to undergo a crisis of faith, a loss of the experience of divine presence. The Quaker way is to trust there will eventually be a way forward. If you keep going to worship anyhow, the familiar ritual might sustain you. You can hold emptiness in the Light—including your anger and your sense of being forsaken—and listen for Spirit, as long as it takes. As Sandra Cronk tells us, inside the emptiness you might discover that the Divine waits, in a form you have not known before.

Finding the Voices

Kirsten Backstrom, *In Beauty: A Quaker Approach to End-of-Life Care*, Pendle Hill Pamphlet 355 (Wallingford, PA: Pendle Hill Publications, 2001).

Shulamith Clearbridge, *Plain Talk about Dying: The Spiritual Effects of Taking My Father off Life Support*, Pendle Hill Pamphlet 479 (Wallingford, PA: Pendle Hill Publications, 2023).

Sandra Cronk, *Dark Night Journey: Inward Re-patterning Toward a Life Centered in God* (Wallingford, PA: Pendle Hill Publications, 1991).

Geraldine Cunningham, personal communication, 2023.

Kahlil Gibran, "On Joy and Sorrow," *The Prophet* (New York: Alfred A. Knopf, 1923).

Judith Goedecke, personal communication, 2019.

John Guiser, personal communication, 2019.

Elisabeth Kübler-Ross, *On Death and Dying* (New York: Macmillan, 1969).

Margery Larrabee, *There Is a Hunger: Mutual Spiritual Friendship* (Washington, DC: Quaker Universalist Fellowship, 1994).

Mary Oliver, "In Blackwater Woods," *New and Selected Poems* (Boston: Beacon Press, 1992). Used by permission.

William Penn, *Some Fruits of Solitude* (1682), as quoted in *Quaker Faith and Practice: The Book of Christian Discipline of the Religious Society of Friends (Quakers) in Britain* (London: Britain Yearly Meeting, 1995), #22.95.

Therese Rando, *How to Go on Living When Someone You Love Dies* (New York: Bantam Books, 1991).

Elizabeth Gray Vining (1952), as quoted in *Light in Hours of Darkness: Readings for the Grief-Stricken*, ed. Dorothy Mason Fuller (New York: Abingdon Press, 1971).

Chapter 5

Circles of Care: Friendship

Nobody, but nobody
Can make it out here alone.

—Maya Angelou, 1975

Your friend is your needs answered... your field which you sow with
love and reap with thanksgiving.

—Kahlil Gibran, 1923

We simply need to be with one another, loving, supporting, caring.
Of course, we live and speak the truth as it has been given to us, but
the business of straightening each other out belongs to God, not us.

—Richard J. Foster, 1981

The afflicted may be helpless to hallow their diminishments, so
consumed are they with the urgent needs of survival and coping
with one emergency after another. In this case the hallowing may
have to be done by those called to respond....

—John Yungblut, 1990

There is nothing I would not do for those who are really my friends.
I have no notion of loving people by halves; it is not my nature.

—Jane Austen, 1818

When we honestly ask ourselves which person in our lives means the most to us, we often find that it is those who, instead of giving advice, solutions, or cures, have chosen rather to share our pain and touch our wounds with a warm and tender hand. The friend who can be silent with us in a moment of despair or confusion, who can stay with us in an hour of grief and bereavement, who can tolerate not knowing, not curing, not healing and face with us the reality of our powerlessness, that is a friend who cares.

—Henri Nouwen, 2004

It may be hard, at times, to find beauty and harmony in the dying process. On the surface, there is often much ugliness, much suffering or struggle, much that seems to be "falling apart" rather than "coming together." And yet, just below this troubled surface, there is harmony—a true beauty that reflects something beyond the immediate circumstances of death. As one person's life comes to its culmination, and others are touched at the heart by loss and love—then, unexpectedly perhaps, we may find ourselves "walking in beauty" together.

—Kirsten Backstrom, 2001

We need, in love, to practice only this:
letting each other go. For holding on
comes easily; we do not need to learn it.

—Rainer Maria Rilke, 1908

FRIENDSHIP IS AN ESSENTIAL PART OF end of life care. True, a primary caregiver and the one in care form a small universe. They are caught up together, increasingly absorbed; one dances around the other. Perhaps it is a long duet, the steps exhausting; perhaps the dance is beautiful or awkward. Regardless, for either person, it is terribly hard to manage the whole dance smoothly without a friend or two. Acts of friendship make it possible for each of them to go on.

Yet if you are a friend, it is surprisingly rare to get a call for help. Sometimes both the partners are simply too tired to make the call. Sometimes pride silences them—"I ought to be able to do this on my own" or "I won't let anyone see me like this." Sometimes it is deeply engrained doubt—"I mustn't ask too much," "I am not really entitled," "We aren't *that* kind of friends," "I'd better not use up the good will, in case I need it later on." Sometimes in the dogged focus on care-giving, they forget that others are in the wings. Even faith can stop people; they suppose that God doesn't send them more than they can handle—forgetting that friendship can be in fact a holy arrangement.

If you are a friend, you might hold back too. Maybe you are thinking, "I don't want to intrude," "We aren't close like that," "Who am I to push in?" "She has a son," "I wouldn't know how," and (especially) "If they wanted me, they would ask me."

If you are waiting to be asked to help, you probably will wait forever. Go ahead and offer. It will be a gift to yourself as well as to your friend. You might discover a new depth of love.

ARE YOU CALLED TO HELP?

How do you know whether to help someone? You discern in the same way you worship: you open yourself to the inner voice. It is there, closer than your own sense of self, so you practice simply paying attention, allowing it. Maybe this is easy for you, or maybe it takes a long while. No matter how long it takes, you realize what Spirit has been patiently, silently asking.

One Friend went to give a dying woman Reiki. Arriving at the nursing home, she read a notice on the door, "Contagious flu—enter at your own risk." The Friend sat in the parking lot in prayer for a long time. Was she called to go inside? Surely not! At last in the silence a soft voice answered unmistakably, *Yes.*

She gave relief to the patient and to the patient's daughter. The story did not stop there, though. She did get that flu. Treating it led her doctor to discover that this Friend had asymptomatic lung cancer. The inner voice had not only made her an instrument of love for others, it also had saved her own life. We never know how our giving will change us, or how the gift will ripple outward.

How do you recognize someone is in need? Worship holds a key. In worship together, Friends come to share the mood, the imagery, and the prayers of others in the room. In meeting for worship and beyond, this is how you become sensitized to friends—the words they do not speak, the appeals they cannot make.

Are you the right person to respond? After all, a message you get in worship sometimes turns out to be intended for someone else. Maybe you are just meant to pass the need to other helpers. But maybe while you fret, "Who, me?" someone already is pointing out, "Yes, you!"

One Friend, sitting in an auditorium, overheard a stranger in front of him murmur, "I have a rare form of cancer." Without stopping to think, he leaned forward and said, "I can give you Therapeutic Touch; would you like that?" So weekly free sessions began, which served as a haven for the sufferer. A rare friendship blossomed, lasting several months before the person died. The Friend came to understand that his "impulse" was the motion of Spirit.

Sustain a circle of awareness around yourself, being open the way you are in meeting for worship. Is his hand trembling? Does she hesitate when you ask, "How are you?" Is the neighbor limping when he walks down your street? In meeting, who asked to be held in the Light? Who has stopped showing up? Who has fallen silent? This attentiveness is not being negative or nosy. You are awaiting your possible cue.

Possible, because your offer of help might be turned down. This doesn't mean making the offer was wrong. Maybe you will ask again later, in another manner, and way will open. Maybe it was enough that you showed you care. Maybe all you are meant to do is hold the other in the Light, which is no small gift. You go on saying to your friend and to Spirit, "Here I am."

WHAT DOES THE CAREGIVER NEED?

When you want to help a caregiver, chances are strong that you will have to do the reaching. A caregiver often is well defended, so don't pester, but don't give up offering. Even a caregiver who is overwhelmed, truly in need of help, probably will fend you off more than once. Don't take it personally. Maybe the caregiver feels possessive of the relationship as time begins to run out. Maybe the caregiver has made a secret bargain: "If I control it all, if I do this perfectly, my dear one won't die."

Most of the time, it is up to you to figure out what is needed. Make your offer concrete. Saying, "If there is anything I can do, let me know" puts the burden on the caregiver. Say instead: "I would be delighted to do your weekly run for groceries with my own. I am going shopping tomorrow morning." "May I please drive him to the infusion center this week?" "I would love to sit with her on Thursday mornings, while you do yoga." "I enjoy outdoor exercise; would you let me mow your lawn?" It is good to phrase the offer as a gift *to* you, rather than a gift *from* you. Always add, "Would that help?" and "I care."

If your friendship never did quite take root, now is a wonderful time to step forward. Be specific. "I have always wanted to know you better. Can I cook you lunch on Wednesday?" "You don't know this about me, but I love to shovel snow." "I don't know why, but I thought of you when I saw this book."

The caregiver almost always needs a break. A break can be as brief and basic as a backrub. Stepping out of the context of caregiving, even for an hour, helps the caregiver return refreshed and whole. A coffee date just once, or once a week, can be a godsend. So can sharing a walk around the block.

If the caregiver cannot leave home, bring a change of scene in. That can be as simple as an upbeat conversation that is not about challenges at home. Laughter is a fabulous scene-changer. You can carry in a picnic lunch from an exotic restaurant, or the fixings for afternoon tea, going so far as candles and tablecloth. (Just be sure to take care of every bit of setup and cleanup.) You can bring a feel-good movie to watch together or later. When one caregiver pined for the beach, her friend brought a jar of little shells, bath salts, and a box of saltwater taffy.

If constant care is needed, offer to sit with the one in care for an hour or more, freeing the caregiver for a restorative break. There is great sustenance in small getaways: an hour's meditation, a haircut, an ice cream cone.

Even a short home visit proves that the social network is intact, that the caregiver is not forgotten. Bring stories and tokens from the outside world. Be ready to promise that your house is way messier than theirs.

Needs fluctuate from day to day and even minute to minute. Be sensitive to the caregiver's cues—a tired voice, a lagging footstep. You will know when to step forward and when to step away.

Being a friend to a caregiver can be frustrating. In this play, you are not the lead but an extra; you stand a little to the side. Maybe you grieve, but your grief is not what matters here. Maybe you really do know a better way to cope or an invaluable resource, but you are not in charge. If asked, you can offer gently: "This is what I see happening" or "You know best; I wonder if this could work for you." Meanwhile you comfort, support, and validate, as far as you are allowed. You simply love.

WHAT DOES THE FAMILY NEED?

When a caregiver is preoccupied with a person in decline, look at the rest of the family. Every member of the family is under stress. All their roles are shifting. They need casseroles—and far more.

Children might need special attention. One Friend recounts, "When I got cancer, my eight-year-old daughter was in need of many things—a new pair of shoes, eyeglasses, someone to play with, and a large dose of tender loving care. She needed someone to pay attention to her who wasn't sick. Her babysitter's mother offered to foster her for a week. What a godsend!"

Another Friend's four-year-old was frightened and acting out. A family friend would take him for overnights and to pet the animals at the county fair. Meanwhile his older sister was having a spiritual crisis. How could God let Mommy die? Was it her fault? Was she going to be abandoned? A First Day School teacher took the girl under her wing, listened, and reassured her.

Adult children who are not close at hand also need your friendship. They might benefit from communication and a reality check. Should they intervene? Should they come? How quickly? What can they expect to see? One Friend whose next-door neighbor became isolated and impaired called the neighbor's far-off son. He needed encouragement to show up, a shoulder to cry on, and a role model for caregiving.

WHAT DOES THE PERSON IN CARE NEED?

People in care can get overlooked and depersonalized. It might look like they are the center of attention, when they are being treated as objects. Medical personnel might talk to the caregiver, not including the patient in a conversation. Someone in a wheelchair might find that no one makes eye contact with them. Children or people who are failing might get left out of decisions and explanations.

The person in care is doing challenging work, as much as the caregiver. Is that work being supported? As the person in care declines, ordinary living requires more and more physical energy. So does the emotional work of remaining connected. Ready or not, the person has heavy lifting to do: the spiritual and psychological work of adjusting to a changing body and situation. And it is expected that all this change will be absorbed gracefully, while remaining thankful and compliant and not "bothering" anyone too much.

Meanwhile, the person's social context is shrinking. People shy away from a person who is changing so greatly. If this is the person with whom you used to hike or dance, your friendship seems on a different footing now; familiar props and prompts are lacking. If this is a person with whom you were never close, you will have to make an effort, looking beyond present limitations to perceive who they were and who they are. And in meeting this person, you will have to be ready to face your own mortality.

A visit to a person in care, carefully timed, is a great gift. You offer either the solid knowledge of who they have been or eagerness to learn about it, and you bring assurance that you value who they are now—that the attraction isn't about the races they used to run or the pies they used to bake, but about their company.

Even a person who cannot speak needs your visit. A stroke victim might say thank you with her eyes. A person on a ventilator might treasure your conversation. A person paralyzed from the neck down might turn his head and lay his cheek on your hand.

Sometimes you will encounter eloquence where you least expect it. Someone "unreachable" might stir when you play a favorite song and start to sing. One person with dementia, asked what he liked, took a whole minute and replied, "I like to breathe." Another instance is a Friend with dementia who says to her husband, "I don't know who you are, but I know that you are someone I love."

One gift you have to offer is patience, especially when someone is slow to respond. Your friend might be confused by medication or distracted by pain. A person with dementia might struggle to understand or to find words. Simply wait and allow and know that your presence speaks volumes.

People in care need to remember that there is still a world out there. If it is allowed, offer a trip into the fresh air, whether it is a drive through blossoming cherry trees or a wheelchair stroll down the street. Being out in nature, leaving behind the stress of illness, can make an enormous difference in someone's outlook.

When this is not possible, offer to sit by the bedside, open to conversation or restful silence as the person leads. Sometimes people feel free to say things to a friend they can't tell the caregiver. Sometimes you will perceive a way to help that the caregiver has missed—a window opened to the sound of children playing, a music app, a virtual assistant that lights the lamp or makes a phone call in response to a spoken command. At the least, you supply a new face and a new fund of conversation, or the silent comfort of not being alone.

Touch is an extraordinary gift—if you ask, and if the person in care is willing to receive it. From a hand resting on a shoulder to a cool cloth on a hot brow to a full hug, touch often outdoes words.

Play is another great gift. If your friend is up to it, games, laughter, and sheer silliness can lighten a heart dragged down by a serious situation. You can play Scrabble on a hospital bed. Remembering how to be happy is wonderful medicine.

True friendship flows in two directions. Help that goes only one way can be tiring to give and oppressive to receive. Therefore, thank the person you help—say why actually it helps you too. "People rallied around me when my husband was ill; I feel so good being able to pass on the gift." "I just love to bake bread, and sharing it with you makes me happy." Express how the glimpse into this friend's perspective and process enriches you. "I am learning so much from watching you cope."

Kahlil Gibran teaches us to "seek [your friend] always with hours to live." Figure out, then, how to include the person in care in joyous events, adapting to lessened capacity, without pressure or stress. One Friend made a temporary boardwalk of planks so that her friend's wheelchair could roll to a wedding on the beach. Another recorded her friend reading beloved children's books aloud; they sent a recording every week to "cuddle with" a far-off grandson.

Feel free also to ask for help in return. Not something taxing or time-consuming, but something that lies easily within the person's power. It might be holding your hand, or a moment of counsel. You might receive little or a flood of love and wisdom. Simply by asking, you affirm that your friend still has something to give and is still important.

You might not have to stretch to find the gift. Megan Carnarius, a Quaker nurse who works with dementia patients, observes that they can be spiritual conduits. Another nurse tells about a Friend who spoke only four words after suffering a stroke and subsequent dementia.

At the rise of worship, he would stand and offer "It is all good." When he was asked anything, if he wanted food or a bath, he would say it again. "It is all good" was not much of an answer—or was it? He has now been long gone, but his ministry still holds power for our meeting.

Many people feel awkward at first in visiting or offering help, but it gets easier. It always counts, whether you are a one-time diversion or whether circumstances draw you close and you form a strong bond. Deep inside, people do take stock of who tries and who disappears. Be someone who tries.

HELPING AT A DISTANCE

If you are not physically present—you are far away, or homebound—you can still help your friend a lot.

Send something personal and lighthearted: an escapist novel, a stuffed dragon, fortune cookies, a favorite poem. Make an "I am thinking of you" call once a week. One woman with brain cancer asked her father not to visit—"But what I really need is to laugh." Her father began emailing a joke of the day. It uplifted her and the whole circle of people who loved her.

From a distance, a friend can set up valuable gifts of communication. You can create a support committee in the manner of Friends that meets online. You can check in at a given time once a week or every day, phoning or texting as if you were right there. You can undertake to manage a phone tree during a long surgical procedure or a vigil. You can gently nudge others who are nearby to do a little something.

You can offer to set up a CaringBridge account. This website keeps friends and family informed without making the caregiver endlessly repeat updates. It is a place to sign up for specific kinds of help: walking the dog, driving a child to soccer, or delivering dinner on a treatment night. You can also offer to set up Meal Train, another easy platform for organizing volunteers to provide food.

Near or far, the single most useful thing you can do is to offer yourself as a listener. One caregiver speaks of two great gifts she received. A thousand miles away, her friend said, "Nights can be hard. When things are bad, call me, even at 3 a.m. I am your night person." Another friend wrote, "I may be across the ocean, but I will always listen. Send me every truth you can't say to anyone else."

WORDS AND BEYOND WORDS

Your presence (in person, on the page, in a text, on the phone) already says, eloquently, "You are of value to me." Go ahead and confirm your admiration aloud. This can be a time when people hardly know themselves anymore or don't much like themselves. Visiting a bedbound, once-powerful man, one Friend said simply, "You know, I have never admired you more." Listening to a struggling caregiver, another Friend said, "I know you don't see it right now, but I marvel at your amazing strength."

Meaningful admiration is anchored in specifics. They can be small: "I made your butterscotch cake yesterday. It is still the best ever." "Can I borrow your baseball joke to start my speech?" "After we talked, I found myself singing 'Oh, what a beautiful morning.'" Or they can be big: "You got me started camping. Now it is my happiest thing to do." "Remember when you told me your secret of strength? It has been carrying me ever since."

But what don't you say? Following the testimony of integrity, do not gloss over hard truths if your friend brings them up. Do not pretend to have answers or to know just what is going to happen or that everything is going to be all right.

There are only a few things that are truly wrong to say—telling a disaster story about the "same" illness, telling someone to cheer up, criticizing a decision, or pushing your religious views. The fact of your caring outweighs just about anything else.

It is not wrong to tell your friend that you are sad. Do not bear down on it; just let there be truth between you. Saying it might open the way for your friend to acknowledge and release emotions too. Perhaps your friend will surprise you with them: "Actually, I am not sad," one Friend growled, "I am furious." Perhaps your friend will gift you with insight: "Sometimes I get through to a place of peace beyond sadness." Neither one of you is supposed to lift the heaviness from the other; just dwell together. And be sure also to tell the counter-truth, your gladness in your friend's company.

You come to your friend with something greater than words. No matter what you are doing on the surface, you are bearing witness. You are attentive to what your friend does and does not say—physical frustrations and emotional discoveries, gratitude, regret, and maturation. You are a willing witness to spiritual contractions and expansions.

In any conversation, underneath you are attending your friend in silence, as if you were a whole meeting for worship. This is the ministry of presence. You offer your willingness to be with the other, even bedraggled, bewildered, exhausted, obstinate, mistaken—the list goes on—and know your friend as holy and beautiful.

SPIRITUAL FRIENDSHIP

An extraordinary way to serve a friend at end of life is to create a spiritual friendship. This is a formal commitment, usually between two people. They need not be close friends to begin with, though the experience, if successful, will surely bond them. They agree to come together regularly, first to worship and then to open their souls before one another. The arrangement can be for a given length of time or as long as life lasts.

According to Margery Larrabee, William Taber taught that "two minds together often provide a clarity that one mind alone in prayer cannot achieve." Within this safe relationship, spiritual friends share radical honesty. They are neither judges nor confessors. They listen deeply and let truth speak through them, without fear or reservation, allowing Spirit to arise. One Friend says, "It was my spiritual friend who regularly and patiently, with acceptance and understanding, would ask, 'Where is God in all this?'"

During a long degenerative illness, one Friend's body was well-tended, but her spirit was in turmoil. She asked a woman in her meeting to try out a spiritual friendship. As her health declined, the two met at first in a restaurant, then in a living room, then in a nursing home. Her friend recounts, "I liked her, but at a distance, so it was a great surprise and honor to be asked. I was with her as she struggled, and I witnessed how she found a stronghold of peace. I was holding her in the Light when she died. It might be the best thing I ever did for anybody."

A WIDER CIRCLE

Another special kind of befriending is to visit people you do not know in nursing homes or similar settings in your community. Many such people have no friends or family nearby, or they have outlived them all. For people who don't have anyone to hear their thoughts at the end of their lives, sharing even with a stranger can be cathartic and comforting. Where such visitation is allowed, you can stave off depression and lift spirits.

Perhaps you will go further, bringing in Reiki or Therapeutic Touch, a companion animal or your guitar. Perhaps you will be moved to become a volunteer for hospice.

Do not jump to conclusions about the people you will meet. Mind, body, and spirit seldom age alike. Someone very weak in body can have a sharp mind and a robust spirit. Someone energetic and outgoing might not live in present time. You are called to the spiritual practice of meeting them where they are.

If you visit repeatedly, you need to let love supply a sense of balance. A person who engages easily at one visit could be lost in confusion the next time, or the other way around. A person you believe is stable can take a sudden nosedive. At some point, you will find the bed empty; such friendships often are brief. Nonetheless they can be beautiful, and you will remember them.

Knock before you enter a room. If you meet in a public area, validate autonomy and privacy by going to a quiet corner. Honor the person's cues for when to leave, and express thanks for their company.

When you visit someone isolated by forgetfulness or dementia, even someone you know well might deem you a stranger. This situation calls for extra sensitivity. Don't surprise someone from behind or from the side; kneel if you have to so you are face-to-face at eye level. Introduce yourself as a friend. Ask how the person wants to be addressed, and wait patiently for delayed answers. Let them address you by any name; one man told a Friend, "No, no, you aren't Nancy. I will call you Beth; I miss Beth." The Friend explains, "So I became Beth whenever I visited. I came to like who I was as Beth. Beth was a sweeter person than I had ever been."

What will you talk about? Take your cue from the other person and from keepsakes in the room. At a second visit you might bring a food or token they have mentioned with nostalgia. Touch only as the person wants, and express gratitude for any gift of an object or a memory.

Watch for clues about whether people you visit are wondering about death. If they want to talk about it, let them lead, and use language that works for them.

Your chief purpose is to listen to stories, taking them seriously. Spirit revives and shines through storytelling. When they are told and received, stories bring past, present, and future together, allow closure, honor memories, invite healing, clarify lessons, and share enjoyment.

You might be amazed at what you learn. A Friend once asked a frail old man, "What did you do?" He whispered, "I was a diver. I helped build the Brooklyn Bridge." Another Friend witnessed the anguish of an elderly World War II veteran, who asked if the Friend thought he was forgiven.

BEFRIENDING A MOURNER

The ministry of presence and the role of friendship do not end with a death. If you befriend a person in care, you carry part of that person's story forward. If you befriend a caregiver, your continued caring is a lifeline.

Unprogrammed Quakers do not have professional pastors trained to work with the bereaved. Your meeting might have Friends with such a background; they can model care, but the meeting should not turn this work over solely to them. Every Friend can offer the ministry of presence. You need no special training. You just show love.

A simple, beautiful way to do this is to speak the name of the one who has died. Keep the person's name and story alive long past the memorial service. After years have passed, it is still a thrill and a comfort for family to hear, "I have a picture she painted in my living room, and it is my favorite." "I'll never forget how he stood right here and sang 'O Holy Night.'" "I know just how she would be grinning now."

After a death, the ministry of presence takes form both in person and at a distance. Take your cue from the mourner. Some bereaved people welcome physical company or crave a hug; some do not. Some mourners, especially those who live alone, find cooking or eating challenging, and gifts of food run out after a week or two. You can leave a basket of muffins on the doorstep or invite the mourner to a home-cooked meal. This is another time when Meal Train might be welcome. If a mourner just needs to retreat, honor that, but do not let the connection slip away. Wait a while and renew the offer of companionship.

You can maintain presence by mail: a personal note, a card with a heartfelt message, a text with a personal memory, or the gift of a spiritual book. This kind of contact does not require the recipient to "perform" in response.

For the mourner, faith in the permanence of love has been challenged. So do not stop with a single card. The goal is not to satisfy your conscience but to accompany the mourner's spirit. If you signed a group condolence at meeting, follow up with a message all your own. Cards arrive in a flood early on, and then silence descends. It is easy at that point for a mourner to feel alone and abandoned. If you couldn't bring yourself to write or call, it is never too late; indeed, a late message might be all the more appreciated.

What do you say to a mourner? Try to avoid comparing someone's loss to a loss you have experienced. This is not about you, and every grief is unique. If you are at a loss what to say, just say that: "I don't know how to make this better for you. I wish I did. Just know I think of you every day." The simplest expressions are best: *I am so sorry. I love you. I imagine this is hard. I am here with you.*

Euphemisms and platitudes are no help, unless that is the mourner's own kind of talk. Most mourners crave plain and honest language. Their loved one has died. The dead are not "lost" and they haven't "passed away." Validate the mourner's truth.

Do not push your own beliefs: "He is in a better place." "It was God's will." Sometimes such words feel intrusive; they express what *you* think, not what comforts the mourner. If the person asks, "Why?" answer honestly, "I don't know." Nobody can know the "why" behind a tragic death. You might just ask gently whether or not faith is a help right now. Take your cue from the reply. If they are receptive, this is a classic Quaker opportunity to fall into worship together.

It might be that the bereaved person finds it difficult to talk. Be patient until the right time comes. Then allow the feelings to pour out—tears, laughter, or yelling—and offer tissues and a broad shoulder. Assure the person that it is normal to have tumultuous and conflicting feelings. A person whose loved one had a difficult death might feel especially isolated and need to be heard all the more.

Your words, in the long run, matter less than your presence. "There are moments in our lives," Honoré de Balzac writes, "when the sense that our friend is near is all that we can bear. Our wounds smart under the consoling words that only reveal the depths of pain."

A widowed person must practice moving in a world of couples; a parent whose child died or a child whose parent died must learn to live in a world of intact families. Let mourners know they have not lost their identity. They are still a spouse, a parent, a child. They are still wanted, included, and valued.

It is not uncommon for grieving people to feel reluctant to live in a world without their loved one. If you hear mention of self-harm, don't panic or overreact. Your friend is trusting you by giving voice to pain. Calmness will show it is safe to process these feelings. Be gentle. Tell your friend that you are there, but that if this is a serious struggle, you can help find a professional counselor. Most important, even if your friend does pursue counseling, don't disappear; continue to make your caring palpable. There are things counselors do that friends can't, but there are also things friends do that counselors can't.

Above all, stay willing to listen over the years. Grief has no time limit. Even the most vibrant person will "fall into a hole" unexpectedly, time and again. There is no limit to accompaniment.

MOURNING FOR A FRIEND

Theodore Roethke wrote a poem about the death of one of his students, thrown from a horse. The most difficult part, he said, was that he felt left out, not entitled to love and grieve. The poem concludes, "I, with no rights in this matter, / Neither father nor lover."

Indeed, though "just a friend," you do have the right to mourn. The pain is no less just because you have no official standing. No one knows all the people who touch you deeply. You yourself might not realize how much you care, until you are jolted by sad news. No matter whether others believe your connection is close or tangential, you know when a loss is real.

There are countless ways to express grief for your friend. Speak the friend's story often. Claim the person's dear qualities to live on inside you. If there are mutual friends, seek them out to grieve together. Reach out to the family also and offer them your good memories; you have a piece of your friend they might not know. With others or alone, hold a private memorial. You can create a yearly ritual: if you always celebrated the New Year together at the Russian Tea Room, make blini in her honor every year on the first of January. Above all, pay it forward in the loving attention you give to friends still alive.

If you shied away from a friend who was ill, for whatever reason, the finality of death can leave you numb or stricken. But if you chose to move closer, helping someone's last years or hours, if you played even a small part in someone's tender time, then it is your tender time as well. Grief is intermixed with sweetness.

Every loss revives earlier losses, and no one really gets "good" at grieving. There are no shortcuts. Neither is it easy to make a new friend, nor are friends ever replaceable. But the practice of befriending, the outreach of your soul, does get easier, and its gifts are deep.

Finding the Voices

Maya Angelou, "Alone," *Oh Pray My Wings Are Gonna Fit Me Well* (New York: Random House, 1975).

Jane Austen, *Northanger Abbey* (London: John Murray, Albemarle-street, 1818).

Kirsten Backstrom, *In Beauty: A Quaker Approach to End-of-Life Care*, Pendle Hill Pamphlet 355 (Wallingford, PA: Pendle Hill Publications, 2001).

Honoré de Balzac, as quoted in David Brooks, "How Do You Serve a Friend in Despair?" *New York Times*, February 9, 2023.

Megan Carnarius, *A Deeper Perspective on Alzheimer's and Other Dementias: Practical Tools with Spiritual Insights* (Forres, Scotland: Findhorn Press, 2015).

Richard J. Foster, *Freedom of Simplicity: Finding Harmony in a Complex World* (New York: HarperCollins, 1981).

Kahlil Gibran, "On Friendship," *The Prophet* (New York: Alfred A. Knopf, 1923).

Margery Larrabee, *There Is a Hunger: Mutual Spiritual Friendship* (Washington, DC: Quaker Universalist Fellowship, 1994).

Henri Nouwen, *Out of Solitude: Three Meditations on the Christian Life* (Notre Dame, IN: Ave Maria Press, 2004).

Rainer Maria Rilke, "Requiem for a Friend," trans. Stephen Mitchell, *The Paris Review* (Issue 82, Winter 1981).

Theodore Roethke, "Elegy for Jane," *The Collected Poems of Theodore Roethke* (New York: Doubleday, 1966).

John Youngblut, *On Hallowing One's Diminishments*, Pendle Hill Pamphlet 292 (Wallingford, PA: Pendle Hill Publications, 1990).

Chapter 6

Circles of Care: The Loving Meeting

In our living and loving and dying I have found much to cherish as well as much that hurts, found growth as well as loss. My hope is that together we can share these things, together hold them in worship, prayer and love.

—Iain Law, 1991

Old age is the most precious time of life, the one nearest eternity.... There are old people... whose radiance illuminates the whole community. They are gentle and merciful, symbols of compassion and forgiveness. They become a community's hidden treasures, sources of unity and life. They are true contemplatives at the heart of community.

—Jean Vanier, 1991

A meeting can provide care and understanding, acting as an extended family. Not only are we brothers and sisters in the spirit, but we may be beloved aunts and uncles of all the children in the meeting. The resilience of the meeting as a nurturing community encompassing many generations supports each of us throughout the many stages of our lives.

—Baltimore Yearly Meeting *Faith and Practice*, 1988

The memorial meeting transformed me. I got to see my mother through the eyes of her friends: both the pain she carried and the grace that shone through it. My confusion finally eased into forgiveness.

—Anonymous, 2023

I loved reading memorial minutes as a younger Friend. They showed me how a Friend could change the world, what our community is about, and on whose shoulders I stand.

—Wayne Finegar, 2022

We have all known the long loneliness and we have learned that the only solution is love and that love comes with community.

—Dorothy Day, 1980

If we are not here to love the world, I don't know what we're here for.

—Janet Harrison, 2023

QUAKERS ARE ALL MINISTERS, RESPONSIBLE FOR one another's care. Together we live out our beliefs. When a Friend or member of a Friend's family experiences aging, dying, and death, every one of us has a part to play in pastoral care. That holds true even if your meeting has a pastoral care committee. This concern belongs as much to you as to the meeting as a whole.

In meetings without a pastor, Friends must be still more careful not to let the work of pastoring go undone. Recognizing the need, we can begin to develop a strong caring response to aging and death. Then those in need will be able to turn to the meeting community, trusting in its support.

In this chapter we look at some forms of communal accompaniment during aging, death, and dying, and afterward. "The Meeting's Role at the End of Life" in the Treasury of Resources combines some key points your meeting can use as a checklist when the time comes. Each act of the meeting expresses the tender commitment that underlies the testimony of community.

Perhaps your meeting will be inspired to try forms of accompaniment in this chapter for the first time. Perhaps it has created new practices worth sharing with other Friends.

AGE WITHIN YOUR MEETING

The testimony of community calls us to sustain caring relationships with all in the meeting, from birth to death. In that light, consider the range of ages in your meeting. If your meeting is mostly youthful, are older people getting left out or left behind? If your meeting as a whole is graying, do younger people drift away?

Do you continue to nourish people as they grow? Do you support one another as you age? A robust meeting responds to the challenges of all ages and integrates people across generations. One way a meeting upholds its older people is to surround them with youthful energy. One way it upholds its younger people is to surround them with loving elders. If a meeting's members become invisible as they age, this is a loss for all.

There are endless creative ways to keep older members included. One meeting pairs cross-generational spiritual friends. One meeting holds bimonthly socials with board games for all ages; another has an annual tradition of inviting the young to an older Friend's home for an egg-dyeing party. Children can interview elders to create storybooks of their lives. An aging member can be made an honorary grandparent for a young Friend. The meeting can create a speaker bank of elder expertise.

Adapting your meetinghouse for older people will make you more inclusive at the same time. Ideally, a meeting has at least one wheelchair available for an emergency or in case someone needs to be wheeled inside. Make sure your buildings and grounds are easy and safe to navigate for people who are growing frail or who have disabilities. Ensure that the acoustics are good for the hard of hearing. For those who cannot drive to events at night or cannot drive at all, set up a ride service.

People who are homebound really can be forgotten. Virtual and hybrid programming makes sure you can actually see absent elders. Often older members give powerful messages online. Some meetings also send groups to worship with homebound elders or those in a care facility. This becomes a tactful way to discover unspoken needs. Perhaps a member would benefit from food exchanges, checkup phone calls, or a workday to insulate drafty rooms.

Be aware that even aging members who seem comfortable might be financially insecure. Some people struggle to keep up appearances, covering shame, guilt, or depression. This is one of the reasons why people "disappear" from meeting.

Adults who have no family and little income sometimes lean on the meeting as they age. This is right and good. Take time to discern what the meeting is led to do, and what lies within its power and resources. Then, acknowledging boundaries, redirect the remaining needs to appropriate care.

As members age and become physically less able, do not give up on helping one another. The help will just take different forms now. You get your able-bodied granddaughter to move the piano. You call Meals on Wheels for a shut-in. As one Friend puts it, "You bring in someone else to hold the ladder."

Older people bring wisdom and continuity to your meeting. But no person, however wise, should hang on to a position in the meeting for years. An ideal pattern is to ask each person, of any age, to mentor a successor. In a healthy meeting culture, one which lives the testimony of equality and the testimony of community, all jobs keep flowing from hand to hand.

The situation of your meeting's older members is not unique. Have they run into a lack of affordable housing or food insecurity or absence of public transit? Then these are difficulties in the wider community too. They reveal potential ways to practice the testimony of equality. They can open your heart to engage the world with social action beyond the meeting.

Thinking big, your meeting might even become involved in creating a *retirement community*. There are four such communities within Baltimore Yearly Meeting alone, created under the care of neighboring Quaker meetings. Philadelphia Yearly Meeting has even more.

What if your meeting is shrinking to the point that it could die? The prospect of laying a meeting down can be a source of unspoken fear and sadness. Older people, who are already losing so much, do not want to lose their home in the meeting too. Ask the yearly meeting for help. Remember also that a meeting is not a building or a schedule of worship. Reassure one another that your commitment will outlast either one.

SHARING RESOURCES

Aging, dying, and grieving are not easy topics to address, but the need is pressing. Your members of every age might be struggling and suffering in silence. This is not the silence of nourishing worship but the silence of isolation.

Start by acquiring practical resources. You can pile forms for power of attorney and living will in plain sight and even hold a fill-the-forms party. You can post a list of lawyers whom members recommend for writing wills, including those who work pro bono if possible. The pastoral care committee can encourage every Friend, especially the infirm, to make a will. Meetings can record intentions for burial and commemoration and keep them on file. A generic form for this purpose, "Wishes for the End of My Life," is in the Treasury of Resources.

Your meeting can also create a library of books and videos about the end of life. You will find a wealth of possibilities in "Readings and Support" in the Treasury of Resources. It is vital that you include books with large print.

If there are young people in your meeting, be sure to adapt end of life resources and conversations for them. Young people need openings to explore the same themes that concern grown-ups. Children are highly perceptive, but their interpretation of age and illness is limited. What is happening to them and around them might be bewildering, and they might be hiding or repressing truths about their family. Because children have less perspective and acculturation, and are more dependent, they are less equipped to process their experience. The concerns of young people will be as strong as those of adults, but different.

Do not keep end of life resources to yourselves. Share them with other meetings and the wider world. Langley Hill Meeting in Virginia, for example, created its own loose-leaf binder on death and dying, which went on to become a springboard for this book. Many meetings in Baltimore Yearly Meeting have adapted material from Langley Hill to help families cope with death. Your meeting might have another piece of the answer.

Several yearly meetings have wonderful resources they are eager to share. For example, the End of Life Working Group of Baltimore Yearly Meeting offered a series of webinars or meetings for learning called "Grace-Filled to the End." The recorded program "How We Die" is available on the BYM website. Their work has generated multiple support circles and interest groups.

New York Yearly Meeting offers another inspiring example. Its ARCH program (Aging, Resources, Consultation, and Help) offers extensive workshops and online forums for Friends and meeting communities "to grow older with grace." (See https://nyym.org/arch.) Local and regional coordinators connect Friends and monthly meetings in person and virtually. Peer support networks based on a model of mutual accompaniment develop as participants navigate challenging emotional, spiritual, and practical matters together. Among the special concerns are caregiving, aging with disability, aging without children, aging while incarcerated, and tiny aging meetings. ARCH has also created a workbook that explores the testimonies, encourages people to talk with loved ones about their final wishes, and contains advance directive forms.

Philadelphia Yearly Meeting partnered with ARCH to create the website Quaker Aging Resources. (See https://www.quakeragingresources.org.) It is being used by a national audience, with the greatest interest in caregiving and spirituality in aging. The compiled resources "uphold a culture of care... consistent with our Quaker faith." In recent years New England Yearly Meeting has also developed its own ARCH programs. All these programs are supported in large part by the Friends Foundation for the Aging.

Britain Yearly Meeting is another good role model for how to create and share resources at the yearly meeting level. They spent ten years on a Quaker Concern for Dying and Death, laying it down in 2017. They addressed how to think ahead, how to make a place for grief in your life, how to work with legal issues, how to keep focused on the patient, how to help people look at their own mortality, and "What about the will of God?" Some of their projects included writing articles for Quaker journals; offering two courses on death at Woodbrooke Quaker Study Centre; hosting conversations about bereavement as a series of losses, with death as the final loss; creating a film project with oral histories; creating brochures on love and loss; using the song "My Way" as a conversation starter; updating Friends' funeral wishes forms; and supporting local Quaker Life groups.

The Friends Foundation for the Aging, another active participant in the wider Quaker family, advances "healthy aging for older adults and their families, grounded in Friends' values." The leadership of the Foundation has been pivotal in networking among key Quakers addressing the needs of older Friends.

OPENING TO ONE ANOTHER

Resources just languish unless your meeting makes time to hold conversations. Group discussion is one safe way to open the topic. In Frederick Meeting in Maryland, a group of retirees who call themselves "The Mortals" has been getting together informally twice a month for years to discuss end of life issues. Herndon Meeting in Virginia has held "Dinner with Death" conversations as part of a Friendly Eights program, or what Quaker hospice chaplain Carl Magruder has called "death potlucks." Many meetings get together in Friendly Circles to discuss death. A casual setting normalizes the topic, taking out the sting. You can find a set of end of life queries in the Treasury of Resources.

Whenever the End of Life Working Group offers workshops, it discovers that participants carry in their hearts unresolved concerns and painful stories from childhood. People recall the way Grandma seemed to disappear, or a baby sister did not come home from the hospital, or nobody explained how sick Daddy was. Such memories from long ago can paralyze.

Open discussions demystify death and help people heal from past experiences of death. They free people to approach these issues in the light of love instead of pain. One grateful participant said, "Now I can talk about death without crying." There is much further work Love has to do among us.

There are many more benefits to such a conversation. It can be transformative; when people talk about dying, they inevitably begin to recognize what is most meaningful in their living. At the same time, the conversation builds community. It opens the way to action, both as individuals and as a community. For example, in one meeting people began to step up to act as medical power of attorney for others with no family. Finally, conversations in meeting become role-play for talking to dear ones.

If people shy away from discussions of death—and they will—remind them that the topic is not cutting off life but assuring a grace-filled, intentional life. It is not about how to say goodbye but how to validate our souls.

Certain topics, such as refusing medical treatment (see Chapter 2), are bound to disturb some people. In those cases, conversation often has the greatest payoff. After hearing the testimony of others, a Friend conceded, "There are more ways to look at this than I imagined." Another sighed, "I am so relieved that I don't have to keep terrible secrets. For the first time, I am free to talk about my desire to refuse life support."

The time will come when someone in your meeting makes a controversial choice. Even if no one is in agreement, advance sharing will have set the stage for holding one another in love.

It is wonderful to bring in outside leaders to teach about such topics; they open the way and stir hope and imagination. But do not underestimate the wisdom already within your community. Each meeting has a wealth of wisdom among its members. Using queries makes it easy to lead participants to their own Inward Teachers.

These issues come closer as we age, so older members often have special insight. You might invite them to lead a conversation. Prize the guidance of those among you who are "on the spot"—who are close to death or physically diminished or bereaved. For example, Friend Evamaria Hawkins wrote at ninety-four, "I am getting more comfortable with the reality of my dying. I want to help others become comfortable too, so I would like to offer a workshop at Annual Sessions." She did, and it was wonderful.

If they feel ready to teach, older people are role models and light-bearers. They show you directly what grace within loss can look like. They need you to support them, and you need them just as much.

VALUING ELDERS

Our elders uphold a beautiful model of aging. They are treasures. In the Quaker world, Friends become *elders* not just by growing old, but by a life of practice, study, compassion, and courage. Over the years they have attained deep perspective.

Elders carry spiritual authority in the meeting. Guides and mentors, they engage at the growing edges of the meeting's spiritual life. They uplift the meeting by praying for it as a whole. In difficult situations they speak plainly and truthfully, with a prophetic voice. The elder asks us to set aside our way and seek God's way, "putting on the mind of Christ." This is not a comfortable challenge.

Elders bring with them the voice of history. Deeply grounded in faith and practice, they carry the past into the present. They remind us how earlier Friends navigated similar rough times and help us recognize how the Spirit is leading us now.

The word "eldering" is sometimes misused to mean enforcing discipline. The true role of the elder encompasses much more than correcting others. Elders deal with conflicts and disruptive behavior in tender and honorable ways. They ask people to seek together. They are empathetic listeners. Kind yet firm, they enable discernment of what is wrong or right. When they are called upon to correct, modern elders do not shame or punish; instead, they offer a gentle invitation to a life more aligned with Spirit.

Often the best teachers and companions at the end of life are elders who have faced a life-threatening illness or accident. They have turned an alarming external experience into a nurturing inner experience. Many small and continuous practices of asking, listening, grieving, resting, praying, and waiting led them onward. They made meaning out of suffering, came to grips with mortality, and experienced divine love that is so powerful, so Light-filled, that they no longer fear death. They can offer their healing experiences to others in grateful service.

Elders are agents of change. They give us a larger outlook. They show us that suffering can be part of a long spiritual transformation.

Elders teach the meeting not to be afraid of mystery, modeling how to wait with trust and how to make room for the sacred. They affirm that all preparations for the end of life are about creating space for love.

How can your meeting show that it cares for its elders? There are many possibilities. Place them on support committees beside younger members. Seek their experienced guidance in troubled times. Invite them to be teachers. One meeting said, "Come tell us how you pray." Notice not just when they are needed, but when they are in need.

Acknowledging someone as an elder calls attention to the person's role in the meeting, which might have gone unnoticed. It also empowers an older person who might be feeling less able and less useful.

FORMING COMMITTEES OF CARE

If you are aging, dying, caregiving, befriending, grieving, or remaking life after a death, the meeting can hold a committee for clearness or support in its care.

The presence of others is a powerful help. It is essential to know you are not alone, and it is vital not to depend exclusively on your own perspective and resources. In time of need, a *care committee* can sustain anyone of any age. Certainly they can be invaluable in the transitions of aging and dying.

A care committee's chief task is to ask deep questions and listen intently to help the individual reach clarity. The committee will see your personal story through a spiritual lens, noticing the larger picture, upholding you, and nurturing transformation.

Group support has a different alchemy than solo friendship. A group shares the weight of a grievous situation. It cradles the person being supported. It amplifies the power of collective silence. It multiplies and pools insights, letting wisdom arise. A group learns from one another's different strengths. Each member might be led at some point to ask a key question the other members have not imagined.

Committees of care are not as well-known as they deserve to be. When one Friend said, "I don't know how in the world I am going to face this cancer," her friend replied, "Would you like a committee of care?" Surprised, the Friend said, "I can have that? Do I need special permission?"

The answers are, of course, "Yes, you can" and "No, you don't." At any point, just as you can ask to be held in the Light, you can ask for a committee of care.

An important part of pastoral care is to let the meeting's members know about care committees. Members might be unaware, shy of asking, or unclear that this opportunity applies to them. Any Friend can lovingly remind another that care is there for the asking.

You can form your own care committee, choosing three to six people you believe will support you well. Alternatively, you can ask the ministry and counsel committee, or the people your meeting tasks with such guidance, to choose a balanced, compassionate group and make sure the group knows what to do. In either case, your committee is under the care of the meeting, which will intercede gently if the committee is not working well for you.

A care committee might convene for one person or include a partner or family. There is no time limit; the committee lasts until all agree to lay it down. A caregiver's committee might begin well before death and continue long afterward.

A *committee of support* walks with you. It meets you where you are, honoring your uniqueness. It cradles your pain and demonstrates that you are not alone. It asks underlying questions and helps you discern your way forward. It brings your truth into the Light. Some groups also provide healing touch, offer practical assistance, or share meals. They fall into spontaneous silence, whether in facing confusion or in savoring clarity. They might close the time together with a group hug.

The committee mirrors the Light within you. One caregiver says, "My care committee challenged me to attend to and grow in Spirit. I realized that when I give care, God is acting through me. Through months of fear and grief, they had my back."

A support committee assures that you feel loved at a deep level. This is the larger Quaker premise. We are living out our conviction that we are one. Drawing closer to one another, we draw closer to the Divine. Having a support committee—or serving on one—thus awakens and enriches the Spirit within.

Members of a care committee accompany you through desolation and fear, relief and celebration. Unlike sessions with a therapist, a support committee is not on the clock, and it often leads to deep friendships that are yours to keep. A group that lasts a very long time is sometimes called an *anchor committee*.

A *committee of clearness* addresses a specific decision. Members pose gentle open-ended questions, reflect back what they hear, and discern together the divine will. Aging and death bring up many crucial decision points. Do I want to accept this difficult treatment? Should I move to take care of my parents? Do I take her off life support?

If someone with advanced illness says, "I think it is my time to die," it is important to call a clearness committee. As Sarah

Gillooly tells us, "Knowing when it is time to allow death to happen is a profoundly spiritual question—one that Quakers know is best answered by the individual in the context of a community of spiritual discernment.... Those decisions by the individual need not, perhaps ought not, be made without the accompaniment of a beloved community."

In the Treasury of Resources, you will find "Queries for Discerning a Leading to Die," a set of powerful questions for use in this event. A Friend who served on such a committee recalls, "It was a challenge, because I had my own history and passionate beliefs. I wanted to cry out, 'Stay! Don't do it!' Serving called for courage, forbearance, and above all, trust in the process. But I knew my presence would never be more important."

Remember that the role of a clearness committee is not to lead or guide; the role is to enable a Friend to find clarity. Though they accompany the questioner, they are by no means responsible for what answer is reached. Also, however loving, a clearness committee sets boundaries for what it can and cannot do. It is essential for the meeting to keep on hand a list of community services, including hotlines and counselors for professional care.

Clearness committee members need to be mindful that there is a long history of coercive practices toward people of color, the elderly, the disabled, and the poor. It is crucial to remain aware of these destructive patterns and to resist these assumptions.

Serving on any care committee is a deep honor and a major commitment. The experience is apt to transform committee members as much as the person on whose behalf they convene. In turn, the bonds created in committees of support strengthen the whole meeting.

One Friend says, "Over the years, I have participated in three clearness committees and two support committees. When my husband was dying, I asked for a support committee of my own. Those are the mountaintops of my spiritual life, the places where I have lived most fully as a Quaker."

More Forms of Care

Some forms of corporate care at the end of life are very simple. One way is to *bear witness*. In one meeting, a family endured a long downward slope to a death. A member rose faithfully during every occasion of worship, upholding their names before those present. For years, he made sure that this family was bathed in collective prayer. Such basic witness is profound.

Yet another way the meeting creates care is to *support leadings* among its members to minister to the dying—as hospital chaplains, hospice volunteers, death doulas, Reiki practitioners, or something else. Practically, the meeting could *release* the person from other duties. It could offer financial support for the ministry. Spiritually, the meeting might pray for those carrying such leadings or offer a support group. Psychologically, everyone in the meeting can give understanding, encouragement, open questions, and prayerful listening. This ministry could be formally recognized with a *minute*, a written acknowledgment from business meeting that the community sees, honors, and supports the person's leading. Among some Friends, this practice is known as *recording gifts of ministry*.

It is everybody's job to see that nobody falls through the cracks. If your meeting has a pastoral care committee, they will keep track of needs, voiced and unspoken. The committee's work is to encourage *accompaniment*. When a need is confirmed, and the best way to meet it is known, ideally everyone in the meeting responds as they can. The pastoral care committee helps members shore each other up as they companion one another.

Of course, the pastoral care committee must practice discretion. For example, when a dying person's wish for privacy conflicts with a caregiver's need for support, the committee must discern how much to tell the meeting. In some sensitive situations, it is kindest for a few to minister in confidence.

The pastoral care committee also sees to it that Spirit is embodied in *practical support*. For instance, it can coordinate making meals, giving rides, or sharing durable medical equipment. Good tools to coordinate such tasks can be found on the internet. Among them are CaringBridge (https://www.caringbridge.org) and Meal Train (https://www.mealtrain.com).

Some meetings have *special funds* to help Friends in times of incapacity, illness, or death. Hopewell Centre Meeting has the Sarah Zane Fund, Langley Hill Meeting has a Family Emergency Fund, and Sandy Spring Meeting has a Personal Assistance Fund. Other meetings simply have room in the budget for unexpected humanitarian needs.

It is common to take meeting for worship to people who are physically unable to go to meeting. A special case is a *vigil* for a dying person. Gathered in a group or taking turns, members of the meeting hold the person continually in the Light. You can hold such a vigil anywhere. If it is at the bedside, you might serve as family for someone who is alone, offer a role model for family or friends, give a tired family member respite, or put your arms around someone who needs to cry.

A meeting with members who love to sing might form a *threshold choir*. With the consent of a family, the choir would gather at the bedside during a vigil for the dying. Singing softly, they bathe the room in audible Light for a peaceful transition.

A vigil is one type of *called meeting*. Anyone can call a meeting for worship with a personal concern, such as illness or despair, with or without the permission of the ministry and counsel committee or the clerk. Meetings for worship can happen anywhere—in hospitals, nursing homes, bedrooms, and outdoors. Sometimes they are spontaneous; sometimes they are called urgently after the news of a terminal diagnosis. Such meetings bring peace as we traverse the challenging terrain of decline and death.

A called meeting can respond also to a grief widely shared. Meetings have been called for COVID, wars, and mass shootings. At Sandy Spring Meeting in Maryland a called meeting for worship about COVID became a spontaneous memorial for a well-loved Friend. We turn to community to grieve collective loss and to trust in renewal.

First Responses to a Death

After a death, the first thing a meeting does is to communicate its loving presence.

Ideally, the whole meeting community takes part in this. Typically, news of a death flows from the clerk of the meeting to the ministry and counsel committee or pastoral care committee, then to the rest of the meeting. Some meetings find telephone trees, Google or Facebook groups, or email distribution lists useful at this time. Then a heartfelt letter goes out from the group as a whole, and Friends are also encouraged to respond individually. When individuals write more than once, mourners feel accompanied and not "checked off."

Pastoral care continues now in a different form. Often a *coordinator* is assigned to link the meeting to the family of the deceased. This avoids overwhelming the family with calls right after a death, facilitates response by all meeting members, and makes sure all bases are covered. The family might ask to work with a certain Friend or Friends.

Through the coordinator, the meeting begins spiritual support and learns immediate needs. Often grief makes performing practical tasks difficult. The meeting might share food delivery, childcare, pet care, laundry, or cleaning. It might help the family communicate the death to others or write an obituary. These tasks call for many hands.

Such help gives the family breathing room. It comforts them to witness how many people cared for the one they loved and to see that they are not alone. This work also empowers the givers, and it draws the meeting community closer together. If family members belong to another faith, sharing the work builds connection across communities.

When relatives travel a long way after a death, they might need housing. Your meeting might have a set of willing hosts, keep a guest house, or belong to a network of homes that take in traveling Friends.

The coordinator also can help the family plan a memorial service or burial. If the person who died filled out a form like "Wishes for the End of My Life" (see the Treasury of Resources), there is clear guidance. If there is no known advance planning, the coordinator can help the family discern what to do.

It is necessary for the meeting to proceed with gentle tact, knowing that people cannot always express their needs, and that depression, pride, or some other circumstance might create resistance to receiving help. Friends' manners of tenderness, simplicity, and efficiency are perfect for these situations.

COMMEMORATION

Acts of commemoration honor that of God in the person who died and comfort those whose lives are changed by the death. They enable family and friends to express grief, remember joy, and craft an ongoing life.

It is important to recognize that the meeting itself might be in mourning. A Friends meeting is a form of family, every member of which is irreplaceable. The deaths of members affect not only individuals but the shared body of the meeting. Worship, discernment, and fellowship will be different—because they were here, because they are gone, and because those who remain now carry their light. In this sense, every meeting for worship is inescapably a commemoration.

Informal Commemoration
There are abundant informal options to commemorate a life. While someone is alive to enjoy it, the meeting might host a celebration of life or "living wake." After death, the meeting could take up the project of sewing a memorial quilt or gather photographs into an album. It might plant a tree, engrave a memorial brick, or set up a memorial fund.

The meeting can also consciously maintain connections. One meeting loves to use "Bob's mugs," made by a beloved member who was a potter. Another meeting enjoys "Pansy's cake" at potlucks, decades after her death. Of course, this means telling newcomers about Bob and Pansy.

A simple, lovely practice is to speak often the name of the person who is dying or has died, retelling stories about the person in meeting so that they remain a vivid, living part of group history. "This is Finny's seat," one Friend likes to say. "I sit here to feel her warmth around me."

Formal Commemoration

The meeting also follows formal practices to commemorate a death. Memorial meetings, memorial minutes, and meetings for remembrance help individuals and the meeting itself move through grief in healthy, grounding ways.

A *memorial meeting for worship* under the care of the meeting is the most common and visible manner of commemoration. It can comfort both the family and the whole meeting. If the family chooses not to have a memorial meeting, the meeting may still decide to hold a called meeting as a balm for its grieving members.

A memorial meeting for worship is held in the manner of Friends, in simplicity, with silent worship. Typically, a clerk opens and closes worship. Because some people will attend who are not Friends, the clerk explains the manner of worship at the start of meeting. People are invited to speak out of the silence. If there is a memorial minute, it is read first.

Even non-Quakers get swept up into this experience. Louise Wilson describes a memorial meeting in which the silence was unfamiliar to most of the 150 people present. "God's love filled the room," she writes. "Hearts were touched as we were drawn close in the Spirit."

The silence usually is complemented by lively vocal ministry, expressions of appreciation, and stories about the person's life. Poetry, music, and laughter are common. Often someone will rise to read words from a person who can't be there. All these elements combine to give thanks for the life of the person who has died.

Each meeting has its own way of handling flowers, food, pamphlets, slideshows, and the like. Some meetings use virtual technology to include those unable to attend in person. These details and more are part of "Coordinating a Memorial Meeting for Worship" in the Treasury of Resources.

A reception after the memorial meeting allows informal sharing, laughter, hugs, and one-on-one connection. This part can be as heartwarming and healing as the memorial meeting itself. One mourner said, "The hugs I got at the reception allowed me to cry for the first time."

A *memorial minute* is another formal way of commemorating the life of a Friend. The minute is neither an obituary nor a eulogy. It is both a celebration of life and a form of historic documentation. It is a spiritual biography about how Spirit manifested in the Friend's life.

New England Yearly Meeting describes the purposes of the memorial minute this way:

> to let Friends know the person, to help Friends benefit from the spiritual lessons of the life memorialized, to give thanks to God for Grace as expressed in the Friend's life, and to comfort the meeting and the Friend's family by honoring their beloved Friend.

Friends in Britain, Australia, and Aotearoa New Zealand Yearly Meetings call the minute a "Testimony to the grace of God in the life of [the deceased Friend]."

For early Quakers, the memorial minute took the place of a grave marker. Every member of the meeting who died was worthy of a minute. For this reason, memorial minutes are a treasure trove for genealogical research, ensuring that relationships in Quaker communities are well documented. Nonetheless, not every meeting writes minutes today.

Typically, a minute includes a warm biography of the Friend as well as the person's relationships to other Friends, the monthly meeting, and the wider Religious Society of Friends. It considers the movement of the Spirit in this Friend's life, what gifts of the Spirit this Friend brought to the world, and what part this Friend played in encouraging the spiritual development of others. You can find guidelines in "Memorial Minutes" in the Treasury of Resources.

Some meetings have a practice of inviting members to write reflections on their spiritual journeys. This can happen well before death or right beforehand. One Friend commented that this process made her aware that she had always been guided, even when she seemed most adrift. This discovery brought her peace. She died three days later, and this narrative became the heart of her memorial minute.

Usually the clerk of the meeting or a friend of the departed chosen by the clerk drafts the minute. It is approved by the monthly meeting and read aloud during the memorial meeting. Copies are given to the family of the deceased Friend. Sometimes families send the memorial minute to appropriate Friends' magazines and newsletters.

If the Friend was active in quarterly or yearly meeting affairs, the memorial minute should be forwarded to those meetings. Baltimore Yearly Meeting archives all memorial minutes and publishes the minutes of Friends who were well-known at the yearly meeting level in its Yearbook.

In the past, religious education committees would print out memorial minutes for the children to take home. Friends who grew up in meeting sometimes talk about how they loved reading those stories. In the spirit of this tradition, you might gather photographs of deceased Friends and their memorial minutes into a binder. Make it readily available, so members can keep the inspiration of past lives tenderly in mind.

A *meeting for remembrance* is another valuable gift to mourners. Grief transmutes slowly at a pace unique to each person, in waves across the years. For this reason, one service at one time is not enough. Because holidays can be especially hard and lonely, meetings for remembrance might be called at times like All Hallows' Eve or New Year's Eve.

This kind of meeting holds mourners and those they love in the Light while they speak aloud beloved names and memories. Each mourner is cushioned by community, and each grief is lightened by companion griefs. It is a relief to express grief long after we are supposed to have "gotten over it" and to affirm the continued presence of those who are supposed to be "gone." There is power in keeping a name alive and holding it aloft.

Baltimore Yearly Meeting holds such a gathering once a year, during its annual sessions. The names of those in the whole yearly meeting community who died in the past year are spoken aloud. It is a moving time when they celebrate and grieve together. Friends Committee on National Legislation does the same thing at its annual meeting. Hospice organizations and continuing care communities often follow a similar practice.

Hopewell Centre Meeting hosts a Homecoming each fall. Many families with members in Hopewell's graveyard come "home" to them. This is in effect a special meeting for remembrance.

QUAKER BURIAL PLACES

Many Friends choose to rest in a Quaker graveyard. This green space can serve as a place of peaceful contemplation and enjoyment for the meeting. Burial there can keep generations of a family together in the context of their meeting family. A gravestone or a plaque can keep a person's name visible for a long time. The graveyard can be a safe, gated space for children to play.

If your monthly meeting has a graveyard, then you are stewards on behalf of the larger Quaker fellowship. Usually, title to the gravesite is not owned by an individual or family. The whole graveyard belongs to the monthly meeting; if that is laid down, title reverts to the yearly meeting. Your meeting might have an endowment or special fund for upkeep.

There are many more Quaker graveyards than you might imagine. Some of them are active, while those that have been laid down remain a fascinating part of history. Some receive only ashes, whether in ground or scattered; some accept conventional burials, green burials, or both.

Each meeting develops its own specific policies about markers, maintenance, fees, and eligibility. Some meetings open space in their graveyards to those who are not members. Whatever your policy, your meeting is encouraged to give a clear, timely, compassionate response to inquiries. This too is an element of pastoral care.

If your graveyard is long-standing, there will be many unmarked graves. Early Quakers used plain stones without names or no stones at all. This was part of their testimony of simplicity—or as they put it then, plainness. It is good stewardship to map the graves and record whatever history you do know. This will also tell you how much space you really have to offer in the future.

In the course of time, even the lettering on stones and the memory of the one who lies beneath will fade, and with them, pieces of the meeting's own story. A loving meeting might walk often among them, give graveyard tours, let the children play there, and keep the stories alive.

Continuing Support

Remember that the meeting's role does not end with burial. Survivors have a long road before them. Grief has no expiration date, and creating a solid new footing can take years. Every member of the meeting is called to remain sensitive and kind.

The bereaved, even those vibrant souls who look "recovered," need extra encouragement to keep sharing the life of the meeting. They are to be gently enfolded and warmly reinvited over time. The meeting continues to be mindful both of the living and of the dead. Should survivors move away, continued contact will mean a great deal to them.

Accompaniment goes on so long as help is wanted. Because death is inevitable, and because we cherish that of God in each other, teaching, preparing, and upholding one another need to be constant practices.

Our life is love. Let us walk in the Light together throughout life's transitions. Living fully as long as we can, dying well when we must, we embrace one another and the Divine. As a beloved community, we grow in tenderness.

Finding the Voices

Baltimore Yearly Meeting End of Life Working Group, https://www.bym-rsf.org/what_we_do/committees/endoflife.

Baltimore Yearly Meeting End of Life Working Group, "How We Die," videorecording, https://www.bym-rsf.org/file_download/inline/597a281f-35dc-4df2-ab44-04e831832bfd.

Baltimore Yearly Meeting of the Religious Society of Friends, *Faith and Practice* (Sandy Spring, MD: Baltimore Yearly Meeting, 1988).

Dorothy Day, *The Long Loneliness: The Autobiography of the Legendary Catholic Social Activist* (New York: HarperCollins, 1980).

Wayne Finegar, personal communication, 2022.

Friends Foundation for the Aging, https://friendsfoundationaging.org.

Sarah Gillooly, personal communication, 2024.

Janet Harrison, personal communication, 2023.

Evamaria Hawkins, personal communication, 2022.

Iain Law (1991), as quoted in *Quaker Faith and Practice: The Book of Christian Discipline of the Religious Society of Friends (Quakers) in Britain* (London: Britain Yearly Meeting, 1995), #21.68.

Carl Magruder, "On Quaker Deathways: Practices Around Death and Dying," July 14, 2022, in *QuakerSpeak*, produced by Rebecca Hamilton-Levi and Friends Publishing Corporation, https://quakerspeak.com/video/deathways.

New England Yearly Meeting Permanent Board, "Writing a Memorial Minute" (2018), https://neym.org/sites/default/files/2019-10/Writing%20Memorial%20Minutes%20%282017%29.pdf.

New York Yearly Meeting ARCH (Aging, Resources, Consultation, and Help), https://nyym.org/content/arch.

Quaker Aging Resources, https://www.quakeragingresources.org.

Quaker Faith and Practice: The Book of Christian Discipline of the Religious Society of Friends (Quakers) in Britain (London: Britain Yearly Meeting, 2013).

Jean Vanier, *Community and Growth* (Bombay: St Paul Publications, 1991).

Louise Wilson, *Inner Tenderings* (Richmond, IN: Friends United Press, 1996).

A TREASURY OF RESOURCES

QUERIES FOR AGING AND DYING WELL

THESE QUERIES CAN PROMPT YOU TO discover what matters most to you. We invite you to reflect upon them alone or in a small group. It is easy to hold a workshop with these questions. Just ask, and responses come pouring out.

Afterward, use your insights to take action. Hold tender conversations about them with the people dearest to you. It will be a gift to them and to yourself.

Feel free to reprint these queries, crediting *A Tender Time* and Baltimore Yearly Meeting.

Getting Older

- How do I see myself aging? What are the gifts and challenges of aging?
- What changes are necessary now? Do I accept and allow them?
- How is my spiritual life changing as I get older? Am I open to grace as my capabilities change?
- Who will I be as the things that have defined me fall away?
- What helped me in the past with fear, loss, and grief?
- Who and what will help me adapt to change now?
- Am I open to receiving care? Who will take care of me?
- Do my legal documents reflect my spirit?
- What support would I like from my meeting for these issues?

Affirming and Letting Go

- What possessions and activities do I still treasure? What can I let go of now?
- Does anything stop me from letting go of things I really don't want? What would make letting go easier?
- Is there someone I need to reconnect with before I die?
- Is there someone I need to forgive, or whose forgiveness I need to seek? Have I said everything I need to say?

❧ Do I recognize the good I have done? Do I have regrets to resolve?

❧ Do I forgive myself?

❧ Do I believe I am worthy of mercy and love?

❧ What am I grateful for? Have I expressed my love and gratitude?

Reassessing My Life's Work and Purpose

❧ If death were imminent, how would I devote my remaining time? Do I want to do that now?

❧ What has been the arc of my life?

❧ How is Spirit moving in me now? What am I called to do and to become?

❧ What work will always be mine? What work am I ready to complete? to lay down?

❧ What has been most meaningful in my life? Am I honoring that?

❧ Do I want to pass on my life's work? How?

❧ Do I want to impart my wisdom? How?

❧ Have I let myself be known? How do I want to be remembered?

Facing Mortality

❧ How have the deaths of others affected me and shaped me? What do these experiences teach me?

❧ What are my emotions about my own mortality? about the mortality of people I love?

❧ What do I believe happens after death? Is there an afterlife?

❧ How does my faith inform my understanding of death?

❧ Do I need help preparing for a coming loss? What form would that help take?

❧ Are people around me grieving? How shall I respond to them?

❧ Am I willing to support others who are facing death? How?

❧ How would I like my meeting to address these concerns?

Directing My End

- ❧ Do I want my life to be celebrated before I die?
- ❧ What are my hopes and fears for my death?
- ❧ How would I describe a "good death"? Where do I want to die? In whose presence? How conscious do I want to be? What would comfort me as I die?
- ❧ How much medical information and control do I want at the end?
- ❧ How do I value my quality of life relative to the length of my life? Under what circumstances do I want life-prolonging care?
- ❧ How will I know it is my time to go?
- ❧ How do I feel about Medical Aid in Dying?
- ❧ Does my advance directive reflect my spirit?
- ❧ How can I help my family be at peace with these decisions?

After Death

- ❧ Do I have a definite vision for what will happen with my body after death?
- ❧ Have I made any arrangements for after death, and told my loved ones?
- ❧ Do I want a memorial service? a memorial meeting in the manner of Friends? Do I have specific requests?
- ❧ What support do I want my dear ones to receive from the meeting?

Queries for Discerning a Leading to Die

MANY PEOPLE KNOW WHEN THEIR TIME has come. They feel a sense of peace and completion. It is not depression, and it is not a desire to leave. It is a simple awareness that "now is my time." Friends interpret such knowing as a leading.

But when a Friend feels drawn to *take an active role in ending life*, it is essential to be certain that the leading is true. The Quaker way is to call a clearness committee. Together the members ask deep questions. In their presence the Friend seeks divine guidance and clarity.

Committee members do not offer advice or press for any outcome. They are not responsible for what the Friend decides. They are simply faithful listeners.

This list illustrates the kinds of nuanced questions to ask. Note that the intended context is when a Friend is facing death because of advanced age or illness. If there is concern for mental stability, it is time for professional counseling.

More important than the right set of questions is the compassionate listening of the committee. This is the haven of love in which the Friend will rest while testing personal truth. Here a dying person can find inner reserves of wisdom and courage, either to go or to stay the course.

Friends in many meetings have found this discernment process useful. Sometimes the person recognized a will to continue living. At other times, the person came to the opposite conclusion, trusting it was the right time to go.

What Is Your Plan?

- Do you have a plan for dying? When and how?
- Have you done anything to set this plan in motion?
- How do you think this plan will help?
- Are you sure, or do you have doubts?
- How long have you been seasoning this?

How Do You Know?

- ❧ What has happened that suggests it is your time?
- ❧ What do you notice that is different now?
- ❧ How does Spirit speak to this in you?
- ❧ Is this coming from a place of love or from fear?
- ❧ Where did you get this idea? Has anyone influenced you?
- ❧ Are you being called? by whom, when, how often?
- ❧ What inclines you to trust this leading? Does anything tell you to distrust it?
- ❧ Has the way someone died influenced you?
- ❧ Do thoughts about an afterlife influence you, and how?

Can You Make a Good Decision?

- ❧ Is your mind entirely clear and untroubled?
- ❧ What is your emotional state?
- ❧ Are you afraid, lonely, grieving? Have you been evaluated for depression?
- ❧ What gives you interest and pleasure now?
- ❧ Does any medication you take affect emotion or thinking?
- ❧ Do you have all the facts? What does your doctor say?
- ❧ Have you been receiving all possible support—physical, emotional, and spiritual?
- ❧ If way opens to more help, might that change how you see the situation?
- ❧ Who loves you, and whom do you love? What effect will your decision have on them?

Do You Need Comfort Care?

- ❧ Are you in psychological pain? Would you benefit from counseling?
- ❧ What could set your heart and mind at rest?
- ❧ Are you in physical pain or discomfort?
- ❧ Do you have sufficient help to manage pain and symptoms?
- ❧ What could make you more comfortable physically?
- ❧ Are you able to sleep?

- Is your spirit in distress?
- What can help uphold your spirit?
- Are your wishes being heard? Do you have a strong advocate?
- Do you feel you are being accompanied?

How Can We Move Forward with You?

- What is most important to you right now? How can you take care of it?
- Is there anything you want to finish? What are you willing to set aside as unfinished?
- Do you have wishes that you want attended to?
- What questions are uppermost in your own mind?
- Do you need to talk with anyone else about this?
- How can you be sensitive to those affected by your decision?
- How do you want to be supported after this? by whom?

Questions as You Approach the End

Are your affairs in order? Are you ready to go? To find out, answer these questions. You might reflect upon them when you are living with a terminal diagnosis or growing frail. You can't do this too soon.

Interpersonal

- Now, while I can communicate, what is important for me to say?
- What is important for me to complete?
- Have I made my peace with all?
- Have I let my love be known?
- Do I want to write a legacy letter and/or ethical will?
- Have I reached out to people I care about? Have I made a list of how to reach them?
- Do I have hopes for my collections, such as music, books, and tools?
- Have I expressed how I want my loved ones to commemorate my passing?

Legal/Financial

- Is my will current? Does my will express my spirit?
- Do I want to make gifts *before* I die?
- Have I designated a power of attorney?
- Do all my accounts and properties have beneficiaries?
- Have I made a wise choice of executor?
- Does my executor have all my financial information and passwords?
- Have I provided for the people and animals dependent on me?

Medical

- ❧ Do I have full information about my condition?
- ❧ Do I have a health care agent?
- ❧ Is my advance directive completed and up to date?
- ❧ Does my advance directive express my spirit?
- ❧ Have I shared with loved ones how I want to be cared for and how I want to die?
- ❧ Do I want to give the gift of my body?

Spiritual

- ❧ Have I shared my spiritual journey?
- ❧ Do I want my meeting's help? Other spiritual support?
- ❧ Have I expressed all my spiritual wishes?

First Steps for Survivors

This is a guide for decisions and actions to take after an expected death. (In an accident, call 911.)

Take Time

___Write down the time of death.

___Take time to say goodbye the way you want, for whatever time you need. This is your only quiet time alone with the body. (Even four hours is acceptable, unless the person is an organ donor.)

Make the First Calls

___Call someone to certify the death.

- At home: call the person's primary care doctor or hospice.
- In the hospital: tell the staff.
- If you reach no medical person: call the coroner on the police non-emergency line.

___For organ donation, call your local Organ Procurement Organization within two hours.

___If you are alone, call someone to stay with you.

___Let the immediate family know.

___Call the receiver: funeral home, crematorium, anatomy board, or medical school. (Mention embedded medical devices.)

Take Care of the Body

___If you wish: set the tone with a prayer or music or poem.

___If you wish: Close the eyes and mouth. Gently wash and dress the body, take rings off, place mementos.

___ If you wish: let dear ones come for final goodbyes before the receiver arrives.

Cover Immediate Needs

___ Ask others for help. Consider: food for the family, pet care or rehoming, money on hand, transportation.

___ If you wish: talk to someone who has been through this recently.

___ If the person lived alone, protect valuables. Some people replace the lock.

Next Steps

___ Find the person's written wishes and instructions, and read them.

___ Call the executor and locate the will (within a day or two).

___ Call extended family, friends, and associates. Keep a list of who was called.

___ Keep another list of people to thank for cards, food, visits, and help.

___ Tell the meeting. You can ask for a coordinator of your choice.

Commemoration

___ If you wish: write an obituary and send it out for publication.

___ Gather printed copies or send links to family and friends.

___ Begin to think about a memorial.

The Meeting's Role at the End of Life

These are some key elements of pastoral care for the meeting to offer as people age and die.

Help with Aging

___Hold conversations about aging and dying, in religious education, workshops, dinner groups, or other settings.

___Create a library of books and videos about the end of life.

___Create spiritual friendships and cross-generational ties.

___Find ways to acknowledge the worth of elders.

___Create a traveling worship group for those physically unable to come to meeting.

___Keep a list of community resources for physical, emotional, and spiritual support.

___Make your meetinghouse accessible. Have a wheelchair on hand. Improve acoustics.

___Stock forms for advance directives.

___Invite Friends to reflect upon their spiritual journeys and their wishes for end of life, and to write them down.

___Gather these reflections into a file for use after a death.

Help as a Death Approaches

___Tell the caregiver what practical, spiritual, and physical help the meeting can offer.

___Listen to the caregiver and the dying person. Fill needs to the extent possible.

___Create support committees for the dying person and for the caregiver if they wish.

___Offer to call a meeting for healing.

___If the caregiver wishes, share the dying vigil.

Soon after a Death

___Send a message of condolence to the family on behalf of the whole meeting.

___Notify everyone attending the meeting about the death.

___Identify a coordinator as a liaison between family and meeting.

___Through the coordinator, assess and address pastoral care needs:

- ❧ Spiritual support in grieving.

- ❧ Practical support, such as food, home care, childcare, rides, or answering the phone.

- ❧ Physical support, such as caring for the health of mourners.

Commemoration

___Ask for plans: a funeral and/or memorial meeting? burial or scattering of ashes?

___Schedule a memorial meeting* if desired. Prepare the meetinghouse and burial ground.

___Prepare a memorial minute* if your meeting follows this practice.

___Record the death in the meeting's records and send the notice to the yearly meeting office.

Continuation

___Make the memorial minute available for the whole meeting.

___Stay in touch with survivors. Continue to speak the names and stories of those who died.

___Offer a meeting for remembrance once a year.

* For specifics, see these checklists: "Coordinating a Memorial Meeting for Worship" and "Memorial Minutes."

MEMORIAL MINUTES

A memorial minute is a lovely way to celebrate how the Light shone through someone's life. Usually the clerk of the meeting initiates this process.

Whether or not your meeting has this practice, you can also use the criteria below for personal reflection. It is marvelous to know how Spirit has graced your life.

___ Choose a Friend or two who knew the deceased well to draft the minute.

___ Research this Friend's life, spiritual journey, and service to Friends and others.

- Read the person's own spiritual reflections.

- Talk to family, meeting members, the yearly meeting office, and organizations in which the Friend participated.

- Collect stories illustrating this Friend's enduring spiritual contributions. Leave out other details, as this is not an obituary.

___ Select details to write about. Consider these criteria:

- How did the Spirit move in this Friend's life?

- What was this Friend's work, and how did it express the Spirit?

- What gifts of the Spirit did this Friend bring to Quakers? to the wider world?

- How did this Friend encourage the Light in others?

___ Write a first draft. It does not have to be long—perhaps half a page. Round it out with facts related to the Friend's spiritual journey and stories that illuminate how the person was special.

___Bring the draft to ministry and counsel committee for editing. Key people in communities where this Friend served might also look it over. Expect embellishments, accept constructive comments, and welcome enrichments. Let it season.

___Take the seasoned version to the monthly meeting for business for approval.

___Provide a copy of the approved minute to the family and to the newsletter.

___Read it aloud at the memorial meeting for worship.

___Send it to the quarterly and yearly meetings if the deceased was active there. Some yearly meetings read from memorial minutes during annual sessions and print them in their Yearbook.

___Store the minute in the monthly meeting archives.

___Forward the minute to the archive that holds your meeting's historical records. In Baltimore Yearly Meeting, this is either the Friends Historical Library at Swarthmore College or the Quaker Collection at Haverford College; information on which archive many meetings use can be found at https://guides.tricolib.brynmawr.edu/quakermeetings/find.

___Consider making a loose-leaf book of memorial minutes for children and adults to enjoy.

Coordinating a Memorial Meeting for Worship

A vital link between meeting and family, the coordinator helps the meeting as a whole respond to mourners' needs. The coordinator's biggest task is to orchestrate the many details of a memorial meeting.

Overall Planning

___Confer with the family. What form of commemoration do they want? Do they want to hold a memorial meeting for worship? (If not, the meeting might still hold such a service on its own.)

___Do they want to use the meeting's facilities for a reception? Who will be in charge?

___Do they want a burial or scattering of ashes on the meeting's grounds? Will it happen privately, or as a continuation of the service?

___Check with the family about their preferred date. Confirm with the clerk of the meeting and the clerk of buildings and grounds.

___Designate who will open and close the meeting.

___Estimate how many people might attend. Is the meetinghouse large enough? Does it have enough parking? Is there an alternate location?

___Send out an announcement to the meeting. Include anything the family wants to say about flowers, donations, and a reception. The family can send the announcement to friends, relatives, and the funeral home.

___Offer hospitality to visiting friends and relatives.

Special Details

___Plan for childcare. Who will provide it? where? who will pay?

___Ask whether any expected guest needs accommodations for a disability, such as hearing assistance.

___Help the family make a printed booklet about the Friend, if they wish, with sufficient copies. It could include a photograph, short bio, words to hymns or poems, and comments about memorial meetings in the manner of Friends.

___Ask whether the family wants particular people to speak. Who will make the request?

___Plan for music if the family wishes. Who will perform, and who will arrange for it? Will you need audio equipment? Will music be at a prearranged time or as the Spirit moves? Is there enough light by which to read music?

___Is a hybrid meeting desired, so people can attend at a distance? Does the meeting have the equipment and someone to operate it?

___Ask whether the family wants a casket or ashes to be present. If so, decide who will be responsible.

___Remind the family that they might want a guest book, a slideshow, and a display of memorabilia. Help them make the arrangements.

___Help the family figure out details of the reception.

Setting Up

___Put out signs for parking. Designate volunteers to direct drivers.

___Reserve seats where the family wishes to sit.

___Identify Friends who will set up and greet guests.

Holding the Memorial Meeting

___Begin with a welcome and an explanation of how Quakers hold a service. This might be the first Quaker meeting some guests experience. Be sure to explain how to know when the service is over. A sample text is below.

___Shortly after worship begins, read the memorial minute aloud.

___After worship, invite people to mingle. Let them know if there will be a burial and/or refreshments.

Sample Opening Welcome

Patterned on the *2013 Resource for Faith and Practice of the Baltimore Yearly Meeting of the Religious Society of Friends*, reprinted in 2019.

Friends, we are gathered here today in a meeting for worship in the manner of the Religious Society of Friends, to remember and celebrate the life of _____. I have been asked to say a few words about what will happen, especially for those who may not have experienced worship in this manner. When Friends gather for worship, we come together sure in the knowledge that God will be with us. You are invited to join in the silent power of this corporate worship.

Young children are encouraged to stay with us for as long as they and their parents are comfortable. After that, children are welcome in childcare, which is at _____.

When my comments are finished, we will settle together into silent worship, opening our hearts to memories and reflections on the life of _____. During this time it may be that some are led by the Spirit to offer a message. This might take any form—a story, prayer, song, poem, or simple reflection. If you offer a message, please stand if you can and speak in a clear, loud voice so all can hear. We will let each message come out of the silence and return to silence afterward, so that we can take it into our hearts. Please do not hurry; we will have enough time.

The Clerk will close the meeting by shaking hands. Let us now enter into the silence with joyful expectation.

CONSIDERATIONS FOR LAYING THE BODY DOWN

THERE ARE EMOTIONAL, PRACTICAL, AND ENVIRONMENTAL implications for how a body goes to rest. Your cultural background will affect your choice. So will spiritual considerations, guided by the testimonies of stewardship, integrity, community, and simplicity.

If you don't know what to do, you are not alone in wondering. Some meetings have working groups to help families explore options. You might also turn to the Funeral Consumer Alliance for help.

CREMATION

In the United States, cremation is the most popular choice. In cremation, incineration reduces the body to sterile ashes and bone fragments.

The appeal of cremation includes simplicity, low cost ($500 to $2000), and flexibility in timing the memorial service. Cremains can be buried or scattered in one or more meaningful places, rejoining the earth. They can be kept in a special place; Friends might choose a handmade piece of pottery or even a unique birdhouse. Your ashes can be saved to mingle with those of someone you love.

One Friend recounts, "Each of us three children wanted to put Dad's ashes in our own garden. At last, instead of fighting, we divided them in thirds, and we all got to keep him. Now we have kindred gardens; he connects us all in a new way. He would have loved that." Another says, "Our aunt's life work was to protect the river. So we heaped her ashes on a little raft of sticks and released them solemnly to float downstream. She became part of the great water cycle. Every time I see a body of water and every time it rains, I feel her presence."

Environmentally, cremation is relatively green. It takes much less land and resources than burying a whole body. On the other hand, it uses about twenty-eight gallons of natural gas and releases about 500 pounds of carbon dioxide into the atmosphere. Metals are often recycled, but dental mercury is vaporized. Units might or might not have air-scrubbing filters to reduce toxic emissions.

The act of cremation itself does not have to be impersonal. One Friend asked the funeral home to call her when cremation of her partner's body was about to begin. Some members of her meeting gathered at that time to hold him in the Light. Improvising a ceremony, they sang his favorite songs, told stories about him, and upheld his spirit for three hours, until his body was ash.

ACCELERATED NATURAL BREAKDOWN

A body can become ash without using fire. Several states allow various proprietary methods of "natural organic reduction" or *terramation*. The body is placed in a climate-controlled chamber under optimum conditions for composting. The process takes from three to ten days. The cost is much higher than cremation.

These methods release less carbon and chemicals than cremation; they require little land, which is a plus in urban areas. The body becomes approximately one cubic yard of earth, which the family can bury or scatter. In New York the final product is defined as soil, with no restrictions on its use. As of 2023, terramation was not yet legal in any of the states in the Baltimore Yearly Meeting area.

Twenty-eight states, including Maryland, Virginia, and West Virginia, also allow *aquamation*, or alkaline hydrolysis. In this process, water and a strong lye-like substance speed the natural breakdown of the body to a fine powder. Aquamation came to public attention when Desmond Tutu chose this method of recycling his body after death.

Some meetings designate a grove or garden to receive ash or soil remains, however generated. There a body's final physical substance is tenderly given to the earth to nourish new growth. A Friend reflects, "I like to think that the meeting's members unite here in a literal sense. It is almost a special form of silent worship."

Conventional Burial

In its full-blown form, conventional burial can include embalming, a casket, public viewing, a funeral, procession to the graveyard, and a graveside service. Such a package can cost well over $10,000.

This elaborate practice might seem to be the default, but globally it is in fact rare. It is popular only in the United States and Canada, and it began only during the Civil War.

Environmentally, conventional burial has mixed consequences. Graveyards use up land, but they also preserve land from development. Embalming entails injecting arteries with toxic chemicals, which eventually seep into the ground. None of the BYM jurisdictions require caskets or embalming, though each jurisdiction has specific requirements for the care of bodies kept more than twenty-four hours out of the grave. Conventional burial is the only option that does not require removing any metals or anything with a battery—medication pumps, pacemakers, and defibrillators.

Quaker custom is to keep a casket closed. Nonetheless, public viewing could be helpful to survivors, especially those who were not present at death. Though several religions prohibit embalming as a desecration of the body, Friends allow it.

In some cultures, a grave and tombstone are tangible evidence of status and caring. In many families, conventional burial is a tradition. A grave localizes a death. It is a physical place to grieve and tell stories. The family plot offers the comforting sense of coming together again, side by side in perpetuity.

Green Burial

Green burial, a traditional form around the world, is regaining favor in the United States. More and more graveyards, among Friends meetings and elsewhere, accept green burials. All states allow green burial in a cemetery, most without further regulations. All but five states and the District of Columbia allow green burial at home, with certain restrictions.

Green burial is essentially a simple form of composting. You can still be an organ donor. The body is washed and set in order, without embalming. The body can be wrapped in any way desired—perhaps as Jesus's body was, in a handmade shroud. Sometimes it is laid in a plain box of wood or cardboard. It is buried within a day or two; if not, refrigeration is necessary.

Generally, funeral directors take care of this arrangement. However, a funeral director is not required in every case. Members of the family and the meeting might be able to take on this tender preparation.

A century ago, Quakers called this practice "simple burial." During his final illness, John Woolman told Friends "that he was not willing to have the coffin of oak, because it is a wood more useful than ash for some other purpose." He dictated and signed instructions: "An ash coffin made plain without any manner of superfluities—the corpse to be wrapped in cheap flannel, the expense of which I leave my wearing clothes to defray, as also the digging of the grave...."

With green burial, Friends can reclaim many pastoral care functions that have become the province of modern undertakers. Historically, religious communities, Friends included, were responsible for the whole process of deathcare. They consoled the bereaved, helped the family wash and enshroud the body, carried it to a place of temporary rest, and dug the grave by hand. It was they who processed to the final resting place, joined in lowering the loved one by ropes, and together closed the grave, one shovel of dirt at a time. They shared this worshipful experience to affirm the person's life.

Lancaster Friends in Pennsylvania have a Care Group that takes the role of funeral director, handling all the legal and practical work of green burial. If this service appeals to your meeting, check whether a funeral director is required in your state.

Green burial is the least expensive and most environmentally friendly way to lay a body to rest. There is no fuel or toxic emission. There is no concrete vault, no artificial separation from earth. In green burial grounds, land can be reused in the fullness of time, so they do not run out of room. The return to earth is fairly quick—within five years. One Friend comments, "This option feels biblical to me. Bodies really do go from dust to dust."

Finding the Voices

John Woolman (1772), as quoted in Phillips P. Moulton, ed., *The Journal and Major Essays of John Woolman* (New York: Oxford University Press, 1971).

WISHES FOR THE
END OF MY LIFE

Historically, meetings were the only trusted repository for all the life information of their members. They created forms on which they gathered nearly everything an executor would need: names and addresses of next of kin; bank accounts and passwords; contact information for the doctor, broker, insurance agent, and lawyer; even the location of the will. They included full information for a death certificate and obituary. Today personal information is usually given to your executor. It is kept in a safe at home, in a safe deposit box at a bank, or on an online platform.

The meeting is still vital at the time of death, but its role has shifted. Your meeting can design a form to collect information it truly needs. This is a sample form.

Name: _____

Address: _____

Email: _____ Phone: _____

Personal contacts and how to reach them (next of kin/partner/ close friend):

_____

_____

_____

_____

_____

_____

After My Death

I would like to lay my body down this way (cremation, green burial, conventional burial, medical research):

_____

I have made arrangements with these providers:

_____

These arrangements are/are not prepaid.

_____

If I am cremated, place my ashes at this location:

_____

If I am buried, bury me:

at this location: _____

along with: _____

with this marker: _____

Commemoration

I want my memorial held in the manner of Friends at this location (a meeting house, cemetery, funeral home, or elsewhere). Please provide details:

_____

Please include these elements in my memorial (readings, music, photographs):

_____

Please accept contributions in my name to:

_____

I would like a reception at:

_____

with these arrangements for the reception:

_____

Memorial Minute

Attached is a snapshot of my spiritual story. For example:

- ❧ challenges and high points of my spiritual life
- ❧ how I followed the promptings of Love and truth
- ❧ how I felt Light shine through my life
- ❧ work in which the Light has guided me
- ❧ my spiritual mentors and influences
- ❧ my spiritual legacy

Signature: _____ Date: _____

READINGS AND SUPPORT

No list of resources can be complete. Our hope is to start your journey and to support a growing conversation. We have vetted this list, but links often change. You will notice, too, that there is a need for more resources about some topics. You are encouraged to create a supplementary list of your own and to share it with friends and your meeting.

GENERAL RESOURCES

These general resources are valuable across many contexts. Some of them are listed again below, under topics of special relevance.

Quaker Organizations

ARCH (Aging, Resources, Consultation, and Help). https:// nyym.org/arch. A program of New York Yearly Meeting. Creates opportunities for caring connection and mutual accompaniment for aging Friends and their loved ones through yearly meeting-wide workshops, peer groups, and one-on-one support.

Baltimore Yearly Meeting End of Life Working Group. https:// www.bym-rsf.org/what_we_do/committees/endoflife. Offers workshops and resources on end of life to monthly meetings in BYM and beyond.

Friends Foundation for the Aging. http://friendsfoundationaging. org/about. Advances healthy aging for older adults and their families. Grounded in Friends' values, it facilitates networking among organizations and supports innovation and leadership.

Friends Journal. https://www.friendsjournal.org. A monthly magazine with many pertinent articles on end of life. Special issues include *Aging and Life's End*, July 2004; *Aging*, October 2013; and *The Art of Dying and the Afterlife*, August 2017.

Quaker Aging Resources. http://www.quakeragingresources.org. Links to Spirit-centered resources for aging Friends. Includes chronic illness, disability, grief, and caregiving. A joint project of New York and Philadelphia Yearly Meetings.

QuakerBooks of Friends General Conference. https://quakerbooks.org/collections/support-in-grieving. A wide range of books on grief, death, and dying for Friends.

Quaker Meetings

Britain Yearly Meeting. *Quaker Faith & Practice: The Book of Christian Discipline of the Yearly Meeting of the Religious Society of Friends (Quakers) in Britain.* Warwick, UK: Warwick Printing Company Limited, 1995. https://qfp.quaker.org.uk. Among the topics are caring for one another throughout life, eldership, bereavement, memorial meetings, and burials.

Honolulu Friends Meeting. *Planning Ahead: Meeting Our Responsibilities When Death Occurs, Including Information for the Survivor.* Honolulu: Honolulu Friends Meeting Final Affairs Committee, 1991. https://pymlibrary.follettdestiny.com/cataloging/servlet/presenttitledetailform.do?siteTypeID=-2&siteID=&includeLibrary=true&includeMedia=false&mediaSiteID=&bibID=9939&walkerID=1708552139921. Sample forms and resources for monthly meetings. This booklet seems to have been the seed document for many other meetings' similarly named guides.

Langley Hill Friends Meeting. *Decline and Death: Planning and Coping.* McClean, VA: Langley Hill Friends Meeting, 2018. http://www.langleyhillquakers.org/death__decline.aspx. Spiritual queries, practical help with planning, and a survivors' guide. The precursor to *A Tender Time.*

Maury River Friends Meeting. *Planning Ahead: A Gift for My Family, and Meeting the Responsibilities for Planning the End of Life.* Lexington, VA: Maury River Friends Meeting, 2014.

A comprehensive local guide with tear-out sheets to help prepare practically and spiritually for death and dying. An excellent model for what meetings can do. Out of print but being updated.

New England Yearly Meeting. *Dying, Death, and Bereavement.* Worchester, MA: New England Yearly Meeting, 2019. https://neym.org/faith-and-practice/dying-death-and-bereavement. The parts of *Faith and Practice* from New England Yearly Meeting on such topics.

Quaker Authors

McIver, Lucy Screechfield. *A Song of Death, Our Spiritual Birth: A Quaker Way of Dying*, Pendle Hill Pamphlet 340. Wallingford, PA: Pendle Hill Publications, 1998. Both a historical report and a personal inquiry into how our Quaker way of living intentionally flows into dying consciously. She concludes that dying is a spiritual birth into a fuller relationship with God.

Ostrom, Warren. *In God We Die*, Pendle Hill Pamphlet 385. Wallingford, PA: Pendle Hill Publications, 2006. Insights on trusting God and finding clarity in our choices at the end of life.

Taylor, Phyllis B. *A Quaker Look at Living with Death and Dying.* Philadelphia: Philadelphia Yearly Meeting Family Relations Committee, 1989. https://www.librarycat.org/lib/VicRML/item/132405076. Topics include AIDS, SIDS, trauma, suicide, and aging.

Yungblut, John. *On Hallowing One's Diminishments*, Pendle Hill Pamphlet 292. Wallingford, PA: Pendle Hill Publications, 1990. A lifelong student of mysticism shares the experience of contemplative prayer in facing many forms of diminishment: birth defects, natural disasters, aging, and death.

More Authors

Butler, Katy. *The Art of Dying Well: A Practical Guide to a Good End of Life.* New York: Scribner, 2019. Practical and spiritual wisdom for aging well and dying comfortably with meaning and purpose.

Enright, Dennis J., ed. *The Oxford Book of Death.* New York: Oxford University Press, 2008. Anthology of perspectives on death, from literary and personal sources.

Gawande, Atul. *Being Mortal: Medicine and What Matters in the End.* New York: Henry Holt, 2014. A surgeon advocates for a medical culture focused on quality of life.

Harwell, Amy. *Ready to Live, Prepared to Die: A Provocative Guide to the Rest of Your Life.* Wheaton, IL: Harold Shaw, 1995. Written by a cancer patient to inspire others to live fully, this book includes a provocative checklist of preparations.

Kübler-Ross, Elisabeth. *On Death and Dying.* New York: Macmillan, 1969. Explores our society's responses to death. A classic based on listening to dying patients.

Kübler-Ross, Elisabeth. *Questions and Answers on Death and Dying.* New York: Collier, 1974. A companion volume to her classic above.

Levine, Stephen and Ondrea. *Who Dies? An Investigation of Conscious Living and Conscious Dying.* New York: Gill, 2000. Shows how participating fully in life is preparation for what comes next. Draws on many faith traditions.

Nearing, Helen. *Light on Aging and Dying.* Gardiner, ME: Tilbury House, 1995. A lovingly compiled anthology of comforting and challenging favorite passages.

Nearing, Helen. *Loving and Leaving the Good Life.* White River Junction, VT: Chelsea Green, 1992. A book of grief, memories, and moving on. Includes a description of Scott Nearing's good life and good death.

Park, James. "Best Books on Preparing for Death." 2018. https://
s3.amazonaws.com/aws-website-jamesleonardpark---
freelibrary-3puxk/B-PREP. An annotated bibliography of
fifteen books. Links to bibliographies on advance directives,
voluntary death, terminal care, helping parents to die, right to
die, and opposing the right to die.

RESOURCES BY CHAPTER AND THEME

Chapter 1 Completing Your Life: Spirit-Led Aging

Arnold, Johann C. *Rich in Years: Finding Peace and Purpose in
a Long Life.* Walden, NY: Plough Publishing House, 2013.
An older person's look at the challenges, consolations, and
delights of aging.

Bianchi, Eugene C. *Aging as a Spiritual Journey.* New York: The
Crossroad Publishing Company, 1984. Positive reflections on
elders, healing, peacemaking, and spiritual opportunities of
advancing age.

Dalai Lama XIV and Desmond Tutu, with Douglas Abrams. *The
Book of Joy.* New York: Penguin Random House, 2016. Two
holy men share their personal practices to find joy in spite of
suffering.

Gallery, John Andrew. *Reflections from a Solitary Meeting for
Worship*, Pendle Hill Pamphlet 469. Wallingford, PA: Pendle
Hill Publications, 2021. Considerations of aging and death
during the COVID pandemic.

Guenther, Margaret. *Toward Holy Ground: Spiritual Directions
for the Second Half of Life.* Boston: Cowley Publications, 1992.
Guidance to support the spiritual work typical in later years.

Larsen, Judith. *Becoming Ourselves: Thirteen Conversations.*
Columbia, MD: The Quaker Heron Press, 2015. Interviews

with thirteen octogenarians, mostly Friends, who share their stories, wisdom, and openness to life's unfoldings.

Morrison, Mary C. *Let Evening Come: Reflections on Aging*. New York: Doubleday, 1998. An 87-year-old Friend expresses both the diminishments and the benefits of age.

Nouwen, Henri J. M. and Walter J. Gaffney. *Aging: The Fulfillment of Life*. New York: Doubleday, 1996. Reflections on aging that reveal mysteries, value the elderly as teachers and prophets, and offer hope for healing and peace.

Palmer, Parker J. *On the Brink of Everything: Grace, Gravity, and Getting Old*. Oakland, CA: Berrett-Koehler, 2018. A Quaker in his eighties explores the growth of spirit in later years.

Peters, Sandi. *Aging with Agency: Building Resilience, Confronting Challenges, and Navigating Eldercare*. Berkeley, CA: North Atlantic Books, 2020. Draws on history, philosophy, psychology, gerontology, and spirituality to understand what it means to grow old in the twenty-first century. Contemplative practices and practical advice.

Plotkin, Bill. *Nature and the Human Soul: Cultivating Wholeness and Community in a Fragmented World*. Novato, CA: New World Library, 2007. A human development model rooted in the cycles of the natural world.

Resman, Michael. "Heaven-based Living." *Friends Journal*, August 2017. https://www.friendsjournal.org/mystical-heaven. A mystical experience of God's love infuses the last years with joy and gratitude.

Rohr, Richard. *Falling Upward: A Spirituality for the Two Halves of Life*. San Francisco, CA: Jossey-Bass, 2011. Insightful perspectives suggesting that the heartbreaks and challenges of youth provide stepping stones to spiritual joys in elder years.

Serkin, Elizabeth. "Reviewing Our Lives." *Friends Journal*, July 2004. https://www.friendsjournal.org/wpcontent/uploads/emember/downloads/2004/HC12-51021.pdf. A life review identifies unfinished business, unresolved emotions, and relationships in need of repair, all of which can lead to finding meaning.

Shetter, William Z. *Some Thoughts on Becoming Eighty-five*, Pendle Hill Pamphlet 418. Wallingford, PA: Pendle Hill Publications, 2012. A celebration of life's riches, challenges, and countless opportunities for growth and wisdom.

Steere, Douglas. *On Beginning from Within*. New York: Harper & Brothers, 1943. Beloved Quaker writes about how experiencing "little deaths" is practice for the big death.

Virginia Office for Aging Services. "Resources." https://www.vda.virginia.gov/resources.htm. Provides links to help seniors with age-related issues.

Yungblut, John. *For that Solitary Individual: An Octogenarian's Counsel on Living and Dying*, Pendle Hill Pamphlet 316. Wallingford, PA: Pendle Hill Publications, 1994. Describes three dimensions of spiritual evolution—differentiation, interiority, and communion. Concludes that a contemplative life is essential to living and dying well.

Dementia

Advance Directive for Dementia. https://dementia-directive.org. Free to download, written by a doctor. Useful to review if you have early-stage dementia—or a family history of dementia and fear developing it yourself.

The Alzheimer's Association. https://www.alz.org. Free online tools to recognize signs of cognitive decline and find local resources.

Carnarius, Megan. *A Perspective on Alzheimer's and Other Dementias: Practical Tools with Spiritual Insights*. Forres, Scotland: Findhorn, 2015. A Quaker nurse who is an expert in memory care shares perceptions of spirituality in people living with dementia.

Dementia Action Alliance. https://daanow.org. A nonprofit national advocacy and education organization of people living with dementia, care partners, dementia specialists, and other advocates. Bookstore, online trainings, support groups, and virtual programming.

End of Life Choices New York. "About the Advance Directive for Receiving Oral Food and Fluids in Dementia." https://endoflifechoicesny.org/wp-content/uploads/2018/03/3_24_18-Dementia-adv-dir-w-logo-no-donation-language.pdf. Another advance directive form designed with dementia in mind.

Felton, Anne. *One Caregiver's Journey with Dementia*, Pendle Hill Pamphlet 477. Wallingford, PA: Pendle Hill Publications, 2022. A Quaker couple finds spiritual gifts in caregiving and dementia.

Kiger, Patrick J. "7 Early Warning Signs of Dementia You Shouldn't Ignore." 2021. https://www.wcbris.us/Dementia/21.05.04.7early.warnings.pdf. Simple descriptions and helpful information. Reprinted from AARP.

MacKinlay, Elizabeth and Corinne Trevitt. *Finding Meaning in the Experience of Dementia*. London and Philadelphia: Jessica Kingsley Publishers, 2012. Offers hopeful stories from multiple people who describe spiritual growth in aging and dementia.

National Institutes of Health – National Institute on Aging. Alzheimer's Disease Education and Referral Center. https://www.nia.nih.gov/alzheimers. Wide-ranging description of Alzheimer's.

Reimagining Dementia: A Creative Coalition for Justice. https://
www.reimaginingdementia.com. These international activists
promote justice, inclusion, and creativity. Programs offer joy
and growth to everyone affected by dementia.

Young, Stacey. "Relating to Aging Friends: Memory Challenges
and Brain Changes." Baltimore Yearly Meeting, March 13,
2021. https://youtu.be/MJKWqa_vs40. A video presentation
by the director of the Center of Excellence in Dementia Care
at Broadmead, a Quaker-based retirement community. Shows
how the aging brain changes and how to relate to others as
they change.

Where to Live

Caring.com. https://www.caring.com/caregivers/senior-moving. A
practical guide to discerning future housing needs. A series of
questions helps decide whether to downsize, renovate, or move.

Friends Services for the Aging. https://www.fsainfo.org/senior-
services. Lists Quaker-related senior living facilities in the
United States.

Medicare. "Find and compare providers near you." https://www.
medicare.gov/care-compare. Locates and compares doctors,
hospices, nursing homes, home health services, and dialysis
facilities. Parameters of quality such as staff/patient ratio are
regularly assessed by state health agencies.

National Institutes of Health – National Institute on Aging.
"Aging in Place: Growing Older at Home." http://www.nia.
nih.gov/health/topics/aging-place. Information on safe ways
for older adults to stay in their homes as they age.

Seniorly. https://www.seniorly.com. A national directory of senior
living communities and senior living advisors, with helpful
planning tools and guidance.

U.S. Department of Health and Human Services –
Administration for Community Living. https://acl.gov/ltc.
Gives detailed help understanding, locating, and paying for
long-term care.

Seeking Spiritual Closure

Bourgeault, Cynthia. *Mystical Hope: Trusting in the Mercy of God.*
Lanham, MD: Rowman & Littlefield, 2001. A contemporary
mystic's reflections on hope. The intimate experience of
presence results in an "unbearable lightness of being" and joy.

Cronk, Sandra. *Dark Night Journey: Inward Re-patterning
Toward a Life Centered in God.* Wallingford, PA: Pendle
Hill Publications, 1991. A Quaker interprets loss, pain, and
emptiness as a little-known path to a deeper relationship with
God.

Dalai Lama XIV. *Advice on Dying and Living a Better Life.* New
York: Atria, 2002. A Buddhist approach to death without fear.
Explores spiritual stages across a lifetime.

Kelly, Thomas R. *A Testament of Devotion.* New York: Harper
& Row, 1941. A Quaker classic describes a mystical way of
being simultaneously in the world and connected to the Light
Within.

O'Rourke, Michelle. *Befriending Death: Henri Nouwen and a
Spirituality of Dying.* Maryknoll, NY: Orbis Books, 2009.
A nurse explores the writings of Henri Nouwen, a Catholic
priest, on death and dying.

Serkin, Elizabeth. "Reviewing Our Lives." *Friends Journal,* July
2004. https://www.friendsjournal.org/wp-content/uploads/
emember/downloads/2004/HC12-51021.pdf. A life review
identifies unfinished business, unresolved emotions, and
unsettled relationships, all of which can lead to finding
meaning.

Smith, Bradford. *Dear Gift of Life: A Man's Encounter with Death*, Pendle Hill Pamphlet 142. Wallingford, PA: Pendle Hill Publications, 1965. Meditations on the meaning and wonder of life, mostly gleaned from the author's personal journals penned as he was dying from cancer.

Urner, Carol R. "God the Trickster." *Friends Journal*, December 2001. https://www.friendsjournal.org/wp-content/uploads/emember/downloads/2001/HC12-50990.pdf. God as taskmaster and helper.

Wood, Horatio C., IV. "Musings on Aging and Death." *Friends Journal*, July 2004. https://www.friendsjournal.org/wp-content/uploads/emember/downloads/2004/HC12-51021.pdf. A retired physician reflects on concepts of a good death. Includes an intimate letter from a man in hospice two days before he died.

Chapter 2 Reaching the End: Spirit-Led Dying

Backstrom, Kirsten. *In Beauty: A Quaker Approach to End-of-Life Care*, Pendle Hill Pamphlet 355. Wallingford, PA: Pendle Hill Publications, 2001. A hospice volunteer listens deeply and watches patients live out Quaker testimonies as they decline and die.

Byock, Ira. *Dying Well: Peace and Possibilities at the End of Life*. New York: Riverhead, 1997. An excellent discussion by a well-known physician who specializes in end of life care.

Dicken, Robert Stephen. "A Simple State of Being that Never Truly Dies." *Friends Journal*, August 2017. https://www.friendsjournal.org/simple-state-of-being. Reflections on birth, death, gathered worship, and a possible afterlife.

Jeffries, Holly. "A Brief Dance with Death." *Friends Journal*, May 2010. https://www.friendsjournal.org/2010044. Spiritual transformation in response to a serious diagnosis.

Kalanithi, Paul. *When Breath Becomes Air.* New York: Random House, 2016. Memoir of a neurosurgeon facing death from lung cancer.

Karnes, Barbara. http://www.bkbooks.com. Website with end of life educational materials for families and professionals.

Moore, Alison. "Death and Dying: A Personal Adventure." *Friends Journal,* August 2017. https://www.friendsjournal.org/death-and-dying-a-personal-adventure. A death doula and Death Cafe facilitator shares experiences to help you craft a personal approach to your own death.

Morrison, Mary C. *Gift of Days: Report on an Illness,* Pendle Hill Pamphlet 364. Wallingford, PA: Pendle Hill Publications, 2003. A potentially terminal infection gifts the author with vivid experiences of each new day.

West, Jessamyn. *The Woman Said Yes: Encounters with Life and Death.* New York: Harcourt Brace Jovanovich, 1976. A memoir about three Quaker women, written by one of them who survived tuberculosis.

Advance Directives

"Dr. Seuss Does Advance Directives: A Tim Boon Poem." The ZDoggMD Show. April 7, 2018. https://www.youtube.com/watch?v=xy-JTh1Vo8o. A fun and insightful video about advance directives, riffing on Dr. Seuss. Illustrates that planning can influence how you die.

Federal Health Insurance Portability and Accountability Act of 1996 (HIPAA). https://www.hhs.gov/hipaa/for-professionals/privacy/guidance/access/index.html#newlyreleasedfaqs. The form that authorizes your health care agent to access your medical records.

Five Wishes. https://www.fivewishes.org/for-myself. An advance directive form easy to understand and complete. Also see its sponsor's website, https://agingwithdignity.org.

MedicAlert Foundation. http://www.medicalert.org. A source for Do Not Resuscitate bracelets and necklaces. The jewelry instructs first responders and also alerts them to medical conditions.

My Directives. https://mydirectives.com. A commercial website that stores directives in a digital database accessible to medical providers who pay a fee.

National Hospice and Palliative Care Association. https://www.caringinfo.org. Advance directive forms and general information on caregiving, palliative care, and hospice care.

National Institutes of Health – National Institute on Aging. https://www.nia.nih.gov/health/topics/advance-care-planning. Practical advice on all aspects of advance planning for disability and death.

Nolo. https://www.nolo.com/legal-encyclopedia/finalization-requirements-health-care-directives.html. Lists rules for finalizing advance directives by state.

Paul, Anita and Barbara Spring. *Quaker Values & End-of-Life Decision Making Workbook*. New York: ARCH, New York Yearly Meeting, 2023. Contact arch@nyym.org. Exercises, questions, case examples, and practical information for choices in light of Quaker testimonies. Includes a health care agent form.

Having the Conversation

Coda Alliance. https://codaalliance.org. Tools for end of life conversations, such as the card game Go Wish.

The Conversation Project. https://theconversationproject.org. Extensive resources to help individuals, communities, and organizations talk about values and what matters most in the end.

Death Cafe. https://deathcafe.com. One model for facilitated, agenda-free discussions on death.

Deathwise. https://www.deathwise.org. A nonprofit organization committed to helping people talk, decide, and plan for the end of life.

National Healthcare Decisions Day. https://theconversationproject.org/nhdd. An annual educational initiative the day after tax day (usually April 16) to encourage advance care planning, with both national and local programs coordinated by citizen action groups, churches, and healthcare providers.

What Matters to Me: A Workbook for People with Serious Illness. 2021. https://theconversationproject.org/wp-content/uploads/2020/12/WhatMattersToMeWorkbook.pdf. A workbook that helps people with serious illness prepare to talk to their health care team about decisions.

Deciding about Treatment

American Hospice Foundation. https://americanhospice.org/caregiving. Helpful articles about multiple medical topics for caregivers and patients. Includes instructive discussions about artificial nutrition, pain treatment for cognitively impaired persons, and use of morphine at end of life.

Arenella, Cheryl. "Artificial Nutrition and Hydration at the End of Life: Beneficial or Harmful?" American Hospice Foundation. https://americanhospice.org/caregiving/artificial-nutrition-and-hydration-at-the-end-of-life-beneficial-or-harmful. A doctor offers objective discussion of risks and benefits of artificial nutrition and hydration.

Blackbird. 2019. This film depicts Medical Aid in Dying. Available at multiple venues.

Compassion and Choices. http://www.compassionandchoices.org. Formerly the Hemlock Society, this group advocates for legal physician-assisted death.

Cox, Donald. *Hemlock's Cup: The Struggle for Death with Dignity.* Buffalo: Prometheus Books, 1993. The origin of the right-to-die movement.

Dunn, Hank. *Hard Choices for Loving People: CPR, Feeding Tubes, Palliative Care, Comfort Measures, and the Patient with a Serious Illness,* 6th edition. Fairfax, VA: A&A Publishing, 2016. Pros and cons of treatments such as resuscitation and artificial feeding.

Dying Wish. 2008. https://www.dyingwishmedia.com. A documentary film by Karen van Vuuren about a retired surgeon with end-stage cancer who voluntarily stops eating and drinking (VSED).

Fowler, Quentin, Barbara Henderson, Paul Henderson, Judy Kessler, and Jill Page, eds. *Assisted Dying: A Quaker Exploration.* York, UK: Quacks Books, 2016. Ethical and theological facets of end of life care, with particular attention to physician-assisted death.

MedlinePlus, NIH National Library of Medicine. Articles about treatment issues for seniors. See https://medlineplus.gov/olderadults.html and https://medlineplus.gov/endoflifeissues.html.

Newman, Ann. "Dying in America." *Harvard Divinity Bulletin,* Summer/Autumn 2015. https://bulletin.hds.harvard.edu/dying-in-america. Describes how economic disparities affect end of life choices. Compares underpaid caregivers with privileged patients.

Rehm, Diane. "When My Time Comes." PBS, April 7, 2021. An exploration of the right-to-die movement in the United States.

"Rosemary Bowen's Fast." January 24, 2020. https://www.youtube.com/watch?v=FpEwH6AKeVA. A video about a patient who chose VSED.

Rosengren, John. "A Son's Decision to Help His Father Die." *Washington Post Magazine*, November 30, 2022. https://www.washingtonpost.com/magazine/interactive/2022/vsed-refuse-treatment-cruzan. A Quaker war resister's life ends when he voluntarily stops eating and drinking.

Schwarz, Judith. "Hastening Death by Voluntarily Stopping Eating & Drinking." February 8, 2021. https://www.youtube.com/watch?v=f2fU9ouCTf8. Video presentation of VSED by End of Life Choices New York.

Hospice and Palliative Care

Andreae, Christine. *When Evening Comes*. New York: St. Martin's Press, 2000. A volunteer's personal hospice experiences in a rural community.

Bell, Karen W. *Living at the End of Life: A Hospice Nurse Addresses the Most Common Questions*. New York: Sterling Ethos, 2018. Comprehensive, insightful guide to all aspects of hospice care.

Fowler, Quentin, Barbara Henderson, Paul Henderson, Judy Kessler, and Jill Page, eds. *Assisted Dying: A Quaker Exploration*. York, UK: Quacks Books, 2016. Proposes a vision for palliative care consistent with Quaker values.

Hospice Foundation of America. https://hospicefoundation.org. Provides programs and information for professionals and the general public related to hospice, palliative care, caregiving, and grief.

The Institute of Medicine of the National Academies. *Dying in America: Improving Quality and Honoring Individual Preferences Near the End of Life.* Washington, DC: National Academies Press, 2015. A pivotal document that broadened end of life choice.

Montgomery County Palliative Care and End of Life Coalition. https://www.mccelc.org. An exemplary networking hub for programs about palliative care and hospice. Promotes education, advocacy, and sharing of information in Maryland.

National Hospice and Palliative Care Organization. https://www.nhpco.org/find-a-care-provider. A registry to help locate hospice and palliative care providers.

Scott, P. S.,"Is Hospice Right for You or a Loved One? The 9 Facts You Need to Know." *AARP Bulletin,* updated October 14, 2021. http://www.aarp.org/home-family/caregiving/info-2015/hospice-what-you-need-to-know.html. Advocates for focusing on comfort and honoring patients' wishes.

Vlahos, Hadley. *The In-Between: Unforgettable Encounters during Life's Final Moments.* New York: Ballantine, 2023. A hospice nurse relates stories of memorable patients approaching death. Compassionate and moving.

Wight, Kate. "15 Best Books about Hospice and Palliative Care." June 2022. https://www.joincake.com/blog/hospice-books. A helpful list.

Experiencing the End

Karnes, Barbara. *Gone from My Sight: The Dying Experience.* Vancouver, WA: Barbara Karnes Books, 2014. http://www.bkbooks.com. A nurse explains normal natural stages of dying.

McCormally, Terence. "What Happens When We Die." End of Life Working Group, Baltimore Yearly Meeting, October 30, 2021. https://youtu.be/S07XmhNeXmo. In this video, a geriatrician shares what happens to the body as we die.

Nuland, Sherwin B. *How We Die: Reflections on Life's Final Chapter.* New York: Vintage, 1995. A physician's unflinching but compassionate look at how we die.

A Time of Ministry

Mace, Jane. *Passion and Partings: The Dying Sayings of Early Quakers.* York, UK: Quacks Books, 2020. A personal and scholarly interpretation of the 1701 book *Piety Promoted*, which collected inspired last words of early Quakers and close groups of witnesses, as if they were messages given in worship.

Moulton, Phillips P., ed. *The Journal and Major Essays of John Woolman.* New York: Oxford University Press, 1971. This edition includes a collection of Woolman's sayings during his final illness and death.

Rogers, Horatio. "Mary Dyer: The Quaker Martyr." 1896. In Linder, D. O., *Famous Trials.* https://famous-trials.com/dyer/2473-mary-dyer-the-quaker-martyr-by-horatio-rogers. A report of how Spirit led Mary Dyer through her trial and death.

Tomkins, John, ed. *Piety Promoted, IN A COLLECTION OF THE Dying Sayings Of many of the People call'd Quakers, WITH A Brief Account of some of the Labours in the GOSPEL, and Sufferings for the same.* London: White-Hart-court, 1701. A collection of the dying sayings of many early Quakers, recorded by family or Friends. Reprinted 2010 by Gale ECCO, Print Editions.

Chapter 3 Gifting the Future

Funeral Consumers Alliance. *Before I Go, You Should Know.* 2017.
A detailed form that organizes information survivors need.

*I'm Dead. Now What? Important Information about My Belongings,
Business Affairs, and Wishes.* Rye Brook, NY: Peter Pauper, 2016.
A workbook in which to write down important information
about your belongings, business affairs, and wishes.

Reimer, Jack, Nathaniel Stampfer, and Harold Kushner. *Ethical
Wills & How to Prepare Them: A Guide to Sharing Your Values
from Generation to Generation*, 2nd ed. Woodstock, VT: Jewish
Lights, 2015. Step-by-step process to leave a gift of love.
Includes nearly 100 last letters.

Virginia State Bar. *Senior Virginians Handbook: A Project of the
Senior Lawyers Conference of the Virginia State Bar.* 2021.
https://vsb.org/site/site/news/pubs/svh.aspx. Overviews and
practical information about legal choices facing senior citizens,
with summaries of specific laws.

Acting as Executor

Potts, Leanne and AARP. "What to Do When a Loved One Dies:
Practical Steps You Need to Take in the Early Days." 2023.
https://www.aarp.org/home-family/friends-family/info-2020/
when-loved-one-dies-checklist.html. A straightforward checklist
of steps to be taken within the first two weeks after a death.

Randolph, Mary. *The Executor's Guide: Settling a Loved One's Estate
or Trust.* Berkeley, CA: Nolo, 2021. Detailed, step-by-step
instructions.

Smith, Scott Taylor. *When Someone Dies: The Practical Guide to the
Logistics of Death.* New York, NY: Scribner, 2013. A framework
for making informed, money-saving decisions.

Social Security Administration. "How Social Security Can Help You When a Family Member Dies." https://www.ssa. gov/pubs/EN-05-10008.pdf. A bilingual site, helpful for the executor and survivor.

Gifting Your Body

Brain Donor Project. https://braindonorproject.org. Connects potential brain donors with a researcher on neurological disorders. Preregister to donate your brain to the NeuroBioBank with this part of the National Institutes of Health.

Donate Life America/Done Vida. https://DonateLife.net. A bilingual website that advocates for organ donation. Register here to be an organ, eye, and tissue donor, or learn about doing so.

Health Resources & Services Administration. https://www. organdonor.gov/get-involved/volunteer. Lists Organ Procurement Organizations (OPO) that oversee organ recovery and transplantation in every state.

Humanity Gifts Registry. http://www.hgrpa.org. A nonprofit organization run by the Commonwealth of Pennsylvania. They accept bodies for research and training, usually in medical schools.

Kelly, Morgan. "Their First Patient: Med Students Mine Wealth of Knowledge in Donated Bodies." August 7, 2006. https:// medicine.hsc.wvu.edu/media/1206/gazette_hgr_article.pdf. Personal story about the great value of cadavers in medical training. Reprinted from *The Charleston Gazette.*

Maryland State Anatomy Board. https://health.maryland.gov/ anatomy/Pages/index.aspx. A form to prearrange donating your whole body to a medical school in Maryland.

Organ Procurement and Transplantation Network, Health
Resources & Services Administration. https://optn.transplant.
hrsa.gov/patients. A public-private partnership that links
professionals and explains how organ donation at death and
transplantation work.

University of Michigan Medical School. https://
myheartyourheart.org. A program that recovers medical
devices like pacemakers, defibrillators, and artificial joints after
a death, refurbishes them, and gives them to patients who
cannot afford them.

Virginia State Anatomical Program. https://www.vdh.virginia.
gov/medical-examiner/vsap. A form to prearrange donating
your whole body to a medical school in Virginia.

West Virginia Anatomical Board. https://medicine.hsc.wvu.edu/
media/1207/hgr_forms1_revised.pdf. How to donate your
whole body in West Virginia.

Chapter 4 Circles of Care: The Primary Caregiver

Acquaviva, Kimberly D. *LGBTQ-Inclusive Hospice and Palliative
Care: A Practical Guide to Transforming Professional Practice.*
New York: Harrington Park, 2017. *Friends Journal* calls this
essential reading to help caregivers examine their feelings
about LGBTQ patients.

Authers, Donna M. *A Sacred Walk: Dispelling the Fear of Death and
Caring for the Dying.* Charlottesville, VA: A&A Publishing,
2008. Scripture-based vignettes of courageous people who
cope with the emotional work of caregiving in a sacred
manner.

Becket, Marilyn R. *Last Touch: Preparing for a Parent's Death.*
Oakland, CA: New Harbinger, 1992. Intimate stories about
how a family coped with dying and death.

Callanan, Maggie and Patricia Kelley. *Final Gifts: Understanding the Special Awareness, Needs, and Communications of the Dying*. New York: Simon & Schuster, 1992. Two hospice nurses advise how to help a dying person communicate wisdom, faith, and love.

Clearbridge, Shulamith. *Plain Talk about Dying: The Spiritual Effects of Taking My Father off Life Support*, Pendle Hill Pamphlet 479. Wallingford, PA: Pendle Hill Publications, 2023. One caregiver's conflicts, soul-searching, reconciliation, and transformation.

GO in PEACE! 2015. https://goinpeacefilm.org. A film by Karen van Vuuren, director of Natural Transitions, about healing the soul wounds of veterans with PTSD.

Kalina, Kathy. *Midwife for Souls: Spiritual Care for the Dying*. Dedham, MA: Pauline Books, 2007. Caregiving from a Catholic perspective.

Finding Practical Support

American Association of Retired Persons (AARP). "Family Caregiving." https://www.aarp.org/caregiving. A compendium of resources for caregivers, including support groups for various illnesses.

CaringBridge. https://www.caringbridge.org. Tool for communicating with friends and coordinating helpers when someone has a serious health problem.

Elizabeth McGowan Training Institute. https://www.mmlearn.org. Online education for care of older adults, with over 300 training videos. A project of Morningside Ministries.

Family Caregiver Alliance. https://www.caregiver.org/connecting-caregivers/services-by-state. State-by-state guides for caregivers seeking resources.

Meal Train. https://www.mealtrain.com. A handy way to organize volunteers to prepare meals.

Medicare. "Find and compare providers near you." https://www.medicare.gov/care-compare. Locates and compares doctors, hospices, nursing homes, home health services, and dialysis facilities. Includes parameters of quality such as staff/patient ratio.

National Institutes of Health – National Institute on Aging. https://www.nia.nih.gov/health/caregiving. Basic starter advice on many issues of caregiving.

Witnessing Death

Martin, Marcelle. "Touched by Death and Dying." *Friends Journal,* October 2022. https://www.friendsjournal.org/touched-by-death-and-dying. Personal testimony about the spiritual dimensions of touching a beloved person at death and afterward.

National Institutes of Health – National Institute on Aging. "What To Do After Someone Dies." https://www.nia.nih.gov/health/what-do-after-someone-dies. Information and options for those present at a death.

Redding, Stephen. "Parting Time." *Friends Journal,* March 2010. https://www.friendsjournal.org/2010027. A story about a beautiful death.

Zimmerman, Shannon. "A Quaker's Passing: My Father's Way." *Friends Journal,* August 2017. https://www.friendsjournal.org/quakers-passing-fathers-way. A daughter recounts the sense of God's presence as her father died.

Grieving

Blake, Betsy. "Weeping to Joy." *Friends Journal*, August 2017. https://www.friendsjournal.org/weeping-to-joy. Story of a spiritual crisis following the death of a sister.

Brener, Anne. *Mourning & Mitzvah: A Guided Journal for Walking the Mourner's Path Through Grief to Healing.* Nashville, TN: Jewish Lights, 2017. Exercises with room to write, following a creative interpretation of Jewish tradition.

Finkbeiner, Ann. "The Biology of Grief." *New York Times,* April 4, 2022. https://www.nytimes.com/2021/04/22/well/what-happens-in-the-body-during-grief.html. Explores connections among grief, depression, love, and changes to the immune and cardiovascular systems.

Fitzgerald, Helen. *The Mourning Handbook: The Most Comprehensive Resource Offering Practical and Compassionate Advice on Coping with All Aspects of Death and Dying.* New York: Simon & Schuster, 1995. Ways to cope, even with highly traumatic deaths.

Fuller, Dorothy Mason. *Light in Hours of Darkness: Readings for the Grief-Stricken.* New York & Nashville: Abingdon Press, 1971. An anthology with passages of comfort for the mourner, including many quotes from Quakers in the UK and US. Out of print but valuable.

Gibran, Kahlil. "On Joy and Sorrow." *The Prophet.* New York: Alfred A. Knopf, 1923, 1965. A mystic's succinct wisdom.

James, John W. and Russell Friedman. *The Grief Recovery Handbook: The Action Program for Moving Beyond Death, Divorce, and Other Losses, Including Health, Career, and Faith,* expanded edition. New York: HarperCollins, 2009. Exercises to move ahead.

Jeffrey, Hannah. "Grief Manifesto: Linda Heacock's Death as Told by Her Daughter." *Friends Journal*, March 2011. https://www.friendsjournal.org/3011026. Multiple dimensions of grief and other emotional reactions after the death of her mother.

Kavanaugh, Robert E. *Facing Death*. Los Angeles: Nash Publishing, 1972. A personal account by a Catholic priest explores mourning in America and complex feelings associated with the end of life.

Pryce, Elaine. *Grief, Forgiveness, & Redemption as a Way of Transformation*, Pendle Hill Pamphlet 416. Wallingford, PA: Pendle Hill Publications, 2012. One woman's way through grief, involving acceptance, self-forgiveness, and trusting her guides.

Rando, Therese A. *How to Go on Living When Someone You Love Dies*. New York: Bantam, 1991. A bereavement specialist offers gentle guidance.

Russell, Hannah. *A Death Chosen, A Life Given*, Pendle Hill Pamphlet 432. Wallingford, PA: Pendle Hill Publications, 2015. Finding meaning and healing after the suicide of a loved one. Wisdom, comfort, and challenging questions.

Upholt, Boyce. "Unaccompanied." *Friends Journal*, August 2017. https://www.friendsjournal.org/unaccompanied. Finding Light in grief.

Watson, Elizabeth. *Guests of My Life*. Burnsville, NC: Celo Press, 1979. A Friend journeys through grief after the accidental death of a daughter, finding solace in the spiritual insights of other writers.

Widowed Persons Outreach. http://www.wpodc.org. A collaborative effort of community organizations. Offers a newsletter, books, podcasts, events, and support groups in the Washington, DC area. A useful model for other areas.

Children and Death

Boritzer, Etan. *What Is Death?* Los Angeles: Veronica Lane, 2006. An honest and encouraging interdenominational discussion for people of all ages, with vivid and upbeat illustrations.

Collins, Sheila K. *Warrior Mother: A Memoir of Fierce Love, Unbearable Loss, and Rituals that Heal.* Berkeley, CA: She Writes Press, 2013. A poignant account of surviving the loss of two children.

The Compassionate Friends. https://www.compassionatefriends. org. Crisis hotlines and other avenues of peer support for people around the world who have lost a child.

Ehmke, Rachel. "Helping Kids Deal with Grief." Child Mind Institute. https://childmind.org/article/helping-children-deal-grief. Simple suggestions to help children cope with grief.

Graham-Pole, John. "Children and Death." *Friends Journal,* August 2017. https://www.friendsjournal.org/children-and-death. A physician's experience of his own child's death, his grief, and how he later helped other children move toward a death in unity with the Spirit.

Huntley, Theresa. *Helping Children Grieve: When Someone They Love Dies,* revised edition. Minneapolis: Augsburg Fortress, 2002. How to nurture children after loss.

National Child Traumatic Stress Network. "Guide to Talking to Children About Death and Attending Services." https://www.nctsn.org/sites/default/files/resources/fact-sheet/guiding_adults_in_talking_about_death_and_services.pdf. Understanding a child's perspectives and needs.

Chapter 5 Circles of Care: Friendship

Devine, Megan. *It's OK That You're Not OK: Meeting Grief and Loss in a Culture That Does Not Understand*. Boulder, CO: Sounds True, 2018. A therapist presents grief as a mystery to honor, not a problem to solve. Skills, checklists, and suggestions for supporting and comforting those who are grieving.

Estle, Susann. "Integrity and the Ultimate." *Friends Journal*, August 2017. https://www.friendsjournal.org/integrity-and-the-ultimate. A Quaker chaplain tells how to be real in the face of someone's loss.

Gibran, Kahlil. "On Friendship." *The Prophet*. New York: Alfred A. Knopf, 1923, 1965. A mystic's succinct wisdom.

International End-of-Life Doula Association. https://inelda.org. An association of doulas who give spiritual and practical help with dying and coping with death. Enables you to find a doula or to become one.

Noel, Brook and Pamela D. Blair. *I Wasn't Ready to Say Goodbye*. Milwaukee, WI: Champion Press, 2000. Includes grieving for a friend. Practical suggestions and empowering strategies.

Smith, Harold Ivan. *Grieving the Death of a Friend*. Minneapolis, MN: Augsburg Press, 1996. A seldom-discussed aspect of grief.

Spiritual Friendship

Larrabee, Margery. *There Is a Hunger: Mutual Spiritual Friendship*. Washington, DC: Quaker Universalist Fellowship, 1994. A Quaker psychotherapist with a prophetic voice encourages deep sharing between souls. Out of print but worth finding.

Loring, Patricia. *Listening Spirituality, Volume I: Personal Spiritual Practices Among Friends*. Washington Grove, MD: Openings Press, 1997. See Chapter 7 on worship sharing and spiritual friendships.

Roberts, Trish. *More than Equals: Spiritual Friendships*, Pendle Hill Pamphlet 345. Wallingford, PA: Pendle Hill Publications, 1999. Clear explanations, personal experiences, benefits, and practical tips.

Chapter 6 Circles of Care: The Loving Meeting

Boardman, Elizabeth. *Where Should I Stand: A Field Guide for Monthly Meeting Clerks*. Philadelphia: Quaker Press of Friends General Conference, 2008. Offers many reflections about providing pastoral care and supporting members throughout life.

Jacobs, Martha R. *A Clergy Guide to End-of-Life Issues*. Cleveland: Pilgrim Press, 2010. Christian guidance for supporting the dying and the bereaved, focusing on transformation.

Jaramillo, Katherine. "A Quaker Approach to Living with Dying." *Friends Journal*, August 2017. https://www.friendsjournal.org/quaker-approach-living-dying. Quaker practices that support declining health, dying, and death in a community.

Loring, Patricia. *Listening Spirituality, Volume II: Corporate Spiritual Practice Among Friends*. Washington Grove, MD: Openings Press, 1999. The meeting as a place of mutual commitment to life together as a school of the Spirit.

Magruder, Carl. "On Quaker Deathways: Practices Around Death and Dying." QuakerSpeak. October 20, 2022. https://quakerspeak.com/video/deathways. An invitation to talk more and to reimagine the end with beauty and connection.

Quakers in Pastoral Care & Counseling. http://www.qpcc.us. An organization of Friends and others who are called into ministry in the areas of pastoral care, counseling, and chaplaincy.

Ratliff, J. Bill, ed. *Out of the Silence: Quaker Perspectives on Pastoral Care and Counseling.* Wallingford, PA: Pendle Hill Publications, 2001. An anthology of Quaker perspectives.

Committees of Care

Friends General Conference. "Clearness Committees." https:// www.fgcquaker.org/fgcresources/practical/practices/clearness-committees. Practical guidelines and other resources about clearness committees.

Palmer, Parker J. "The Clearness Committee: A Communal Approach to Discernment." The Center for Courage & Renewal. 2022. https://couragerenewal.org/wp-content/ uploads/2022/06/Parker-Palmer_Clearness-Committee.pdf. Concise explanation and guidelines for clearness committee process.

Palmer, Parker J. *A Hidden Wholeness: The Journey Toward an Undivided Life.* San Francisco, CA: Jossey-Bass, 2009. How to create clearness committees and circles of trust, which enable each person in the group to find the Inward Teacher.

Commemoration

Britain Yearly Meeting. "Funerals, Memorial Meetings, and Dying." https://www.quaker.org.uk/communities/quaker-worship/funerals-1. Useful advice about how British meetings approach these issues.

New England Yearly Meeting. "Guidance for Friends about Death, Dying and Bereavement." *Faith and Practice of New England Yearly Meeting of Friends.* Worcester, MA: New England Yearly Meeting, 2019. https://neym.org/faith-and-practice/appendices/death-dying-7. Covers health care planning, final decisions, memorial meetings, and memorial minutes.

New England Yearly Meeting. "Writing Memorial Minutes. Draft of guidelines." 2017. https://neym.org/sites/default/files/2019-10/Writing%20Memorial%20Minutes%20%282017%29.pdf.

Philadelphia Yearly Meeting. "The Conduct of Funerals for Friends." 1983. https://pymlibrary.follettdestiny.com/cataloging/servlet/presenttitledetailform.do?siteTypeID=-2&siteID=&includeLibrary=true&includeMedia=false&mediaSiteID=&bibID=826&walkerID=1708552065683. Pamphlet for those unfamiliar with memorial meetings in the manner of Friends.

Thompson, Grant. "On Writing Memorial Minutes." Washington, DC: Friends Meeting of Washington, 1983. https://quakersdc.org/sites/default/files/On%20Writing%20a%20Memorial%20Minute.pdf.

Burials

Acciavatti, Michelle et al. *Home Funerals: Guide and Resources.* Everett, WA: National Home Funeral Alliance, 2023. https://www.homefuneralalliance.org. Support and education for the home funeral movement.

Crossings: Caring for Our Own at Death. http://www.crossings.net. Home funeral and green burial resource center based in Maryland. Workshops, tools, and direct support for individual families.

Eden, Margalo and Wendy Lyons, eds. *Undertaken with Love: A Home Funeral Guide for Congregations and Communities.* Morrisville, NC: Lulu Press, 2009. A training guide. Includes preparing for burial or cremation, navigating legal aspects, and maintaining an effective home funeral committee.

Fournier, Elizabeth. *The Green Burial Guidebook: Everything You Need to Plan an Affordable, Environmentally Friendly Burial.* Novato, CA: New World Library, 2018. A funeral home director explains environmental, financial, legal, and practical aspects of a green burial.

Funeral Consumers Alliance. https://funerals.org. Sometimes referred to as the *Consumer Reports* of funerals. A national nonprofit with affiliates in each state. Unbiased information for planning funerals and comparing prices. The bookstore has many resources.

Green Burial Council. https://www.greenburialcouncil.org. Certifies and promotes providers and supplies detailed information for the general public. Lists green cemeteries in the BYM region.

Heller, Karen. "The Stunning Rise of Cremation Reveals America's Changing Idea of Death." *Washington Post*, April 18, 2022. https://www.washingtonpost.com/lifestyle/2022/04/18/cremation-death-funeral. An examination of cremation, its prevalence, and emerging alternatives.

Lancaster Friends Meeting: Care Group for Death and Dying. Provides funeral services (care of the body, burial, and memorial services) in the traditional manner of Friends for meeting members and attenders. A wonderful role model and resource for other meetings. Contact lancasterpaquakers2@gmail.com or 717-392-2762.

Last Things: Alternatives at the End of Life. "Maine's Home Funeral Resource." https://www.lastthings.net. Comprehensive, widely applicable resources for home funerals and burials. Includes plans for homemade coffins and shrouds.

Morgan, Ernest. *Dealing Creatively with Death: A Manual of Death Education and Simple Burial*, 14th edition. Hinesville, VT: Upper Access, 2010. The quintessential book on green burials, by a Quaker.

Natural Transitions. http://www.naturaltransitions.org. A monthly online community gathering and a magazine about green and holistic approaches to end of life.

Oliveto, Joe. "How to Build Your Own Casket." https://www.joincake.com/blog/build-your-own-casket. Practical guidance for DIYers, including links for plans and options for low-cost purchase.

Slocum, Joshua and Lisa Carlson. *Final Rights: Reclaiming the American Way of Death*. Hinesburg, VT: Upper Access, 2021. Raises consumer protection issues alongside state-by-state information about arranging a funeral.

Vulliamy, Colwyn. *Immortality: Funeral Rites and Customs*. Rickmansworth, UK: Senate, 1997. Approaches to death and life after death across history and around the world.

Index

W

www.ingramcontent.com/pod-product-compliance
Lightning Source LLC
Chambersburg PA
CBHW062057080426
42734CB00012B/2682